PATRICK W. COLLINS

Bodying Forth

Aesthetic Liturgy

"Imagination bodies forth the forms of things unknown"
(Shakespeare, *A Midsummer Night's Dream,* Act V, Scene I)

PAULIST PRESS
New York/Mahwah, N.J.

Library of Congress Cataloging-in-Publication Data

Collins, Patrick W.
    Bodying forth : aesthetic liturgy / by Patrick W. Collins.
      p. cm.
    Includes bibliographical references and index.
    ISBN 0-8091-3352-0 (pbk.)
    1. Catholic Church—Liturgy. I. Title.
BX1970.C657 1992
264'.02—dc20
                                                 92-28045
                                                   CIP

Published by Paulist Press
997 Macarthur Boulevard
Mahwah, New Jersey 07430

Printed and bound in the
United States of America

Contents

PART IV:
LITURGICAL MINISTRIES

DEDICATED TO

The Most Reverend Edward W. O'Rourke, D.D
Bishop of Peoria (1971–1990)
and
The People of God of the Diocese of Peoria
who helped me to understand and to love
the art of ritual
during the time in which I served them
as Diocesan Director of Worship and Music
1979–1987

Foreword

Because liturgy deals so much with symbols it opens our imagination to multiple layers of interpretations. But symbols can be destroyed when they are interpreted, no longer as symbols, but as metaphysical laws.

A story is told in the life of the composer Robert Schumann that illustrates this point. He had just finished a new composition and had played it for an august university crowd of admirers. Someone asked: "But what exactly does it mean?" Schumann, in response said: "It means exactly this: . . ." And then he played the piece over again. One can write books about liturgy from many points of view, but one must experience it first and then analyze it by keeping within the laws of its own symbolic logic.

Father Patrick Collins does just that. Having worked in this field for many, many years he is able to bring much valuable experience to analyzing those symbolic acts that make up our liturgy and not destroy them in the process nor reduce them to rubrics or metaphysical analysis. That they are symbols does not mean that one can just do with them what one wants. They follow their own symbolic logic, and that, too, must be analyzed.

Perhaps the most important point about liturgy is that it must be symbolically the bearer of the transcendent. For the symbol to be of significance it must relate to the divine and at the same time be truly our human act. Instrumentality or mediated grace is very much a part of our Catholic tradition and finds its focal point in the liturgy. Memory and imagination play important roles in that correlation between the human and the divine in the act of faith. Not everyone can talk about those relationships in intelligent and convincing fashion. As in his previous writings, Father Collins brings much lived experience to these issues.

Perhaps there is no element so important, yet so neglected, in this whole discussion of the transcendent and the symbolic nature of liturgy, as the role of the aesthetic experience. The Catholic Church has always felt the importance of that element in its liturgical celebrations. The aesthetic experience can be the instrument that assists the leap of faith that is so important on the part of the worshiper at liturgy.

St. Benedict already knew of this dimension. Although he is at pains to see that no one in community life is put ahead of another for extrinsic reasons, and that no one is preferred to another, yet he drops such an egalitarian concept when it comes to liturgy. Here only those who are able to edify their listeners are judged worthy to intone and sing the psalms. They must be able—and he uses these words after much thought and deliberation—to edify the listeners. That word "edify" in its Latin root means to build up; that is, the way the monk performs his role in the liturgy must assist in building up the faith dimension of the worshipers. From that simple phrase of Benedict there grew up the monastic tradition that rightly saw in beauty and the aesthetic experience a vehicle of the transcendent. Throughout history monks have not been hesitant to use the best in music and art to make sure that the faith of the monks would be built up.

In the last century in particular, most "converts" to Catholicism joined that faith expression because of the aesthetic dimension of the Catholic liturgy. Catholic worship attempted to use the aesthetic experience as an aid to the believer in seeking a rapport with the divine or the transcendent. If an evangelization program, of which we have a proliferation today, had been instituted by the American bishops a century and a half ago, it would have started with an intensification of this aesthetic dimension of its liturgy. Today such an insight is totally lost. It is a part of the Catholic heritage that must be recouped. Works like this one will do much to stimulate a valid discussion about this integral element in Catholic tradition.

It is true that some have substituted the aesthetic experience for that of faith itself, making art a religion unto itself, *ars gratia artis*. But such instances are rare and should not deter the church from seeing in the aesthetic experience an instrument, an aid, in helping people to relate to God and to the holy.

But the liturgy is made up of a multitude of acts that also relate to the life, sufferings, death and resurrection of Jesus Christ and to the sending of the Holy Spirit at Pentecost. This narrative and historical dimension is also important, especially as it relates to the here and now and to the future. All those acts and words in liturgy form a whole and take their place within the total structure. Father Collins, thus, wisely brings his years of experience to bear on his discussion of the role of all the parts of the liturgical rite, especially of the eucharist, and how they relate to the meaning of the whole. Much wisdom and many helpful insights result.

If, in our day—some quarter of a century after the liturgical reforms of Vatican Council II—there seems to be a return to a new rubricism in the church, since some see in such a tendency an assurance of orthodoxy and validity, it is good to be forced to reflect on the symbolic nature of the acts in question and to keep the discussion on that more profound level. It is also more in keeping with what liturgy really is. Writings and reflections such as are found in this book will help us to respect the symbolic nature of the liturgical acts and to keep our discussion about them in those categories where they belong. Rubrics will not be unimportant but seen as essential to the symbol itself. If we do not keep the symbolic nature of liturgy in mind, however, then we can fall into the pre-Vatican II tendency of making liturgy a rubrical exercise, a very dead act as far as the essential symbols are concerned. Such a rubrical tendency that can lead to dead symbols is most serious because for us believers liturgy is a matter of spiritual life or death.

On the other hand, it is also important that we do not lose the Catholic tradition of seeing the relationship between the aesthetic experience and the liturgical symbol. Because we see in the liturgy an encounter with the transcendent or the divine and not just a purely human relationship, we want to use all the aids we can in that instrumentality. The aesthetic experience has been seen as a powerful help to the faith leap, especially in communal liturgical prayer. If that tradition has waned since Vatican Council II—and I would estimate that it has—then it is time to rethink that aspect of the liturgical reform. This work will help to put such discussion and implementation on a correct basis. Liturgy is too important to leave it to the whim of a few, or to well-meaning amateurs.

Most Reverend Rembert G. Weakland, O.S.B.
Archbishop of Milwaukee
September 4, 1992

Preface

"Just what do you think you are doing?" My mother some-times confronted me with those all too familiar words when my behavior would be at least somewhat questionable. That question might well be asked of each one who ministers in the liturgical assembly as well as of the worshiping assembly itself. Since the Vatican II liturgical reform and renewal, there are at least some things about our ritual behavior that are indeed questionable!

"Just what do we think we are doing when we gather for worship?" William Shakespeare's poetic phrase can point us to-ward the proper path:

> The lunatic, the lover, and the poet,
> Are of imagination all compact:
> One sees more devils than vast hell can hold,
> That is the madman; the lover, all as frantic,
> Sees Helen's beauty in a brow of Egypt:
> The poet's eye, in a fine frenzy rolling,
> Doth glance from heaven to earth, from earth to heaven;
> And, *as imagination bodies forth*
> *The forms of things unknown,* [italics added] the poet's pen
> Turns them to shapes, and gives to airy nothing
> A local habitation and a name.
> (*A Midsummer Night's Dream,* Act V, Scene I)

Bodying forth things unknown in forms of imagination: that's what we *ought* to be doing when we assemble for worship, glancing from heaven to earth and earth to heaven. The "things unknown" are affairs of the God's kingdom, a reign which is both *in* yet *not of* this world. Such aesthetic ritual forms have the power both to curb

1

the "lunatic" within us as well as to create the "lover" within us—all with poetic embodiments, ritual enactments of beauty.

I became a convert to the Roman Catholic Church in 1954—well before Vatican II! One of the instruments of God's grace which drew me in the Catholic direction was the liturgy. The beauty of the ritual, the sense of awe in the sacred space, the reverence of the people, the mystic chants—all of these elements of ritual eventually made me feel right at home in the Roman Catholic community.

This was not the case initially, however, in 1952. At that time I was a high school lad who served as assistant organist at my church, the Congregational Church in Wyoming, Illinois. During my junior year, I was invited by my second-grade teacher, Bernice O'Neill Dancer, the St. Dominic's Catholic Church organist, to learn how to play and sing for the daily requiem masses so that she and her two sisters could take a summer vacation in Alaska. She did not want to deprive the pastor, Father Edmund J. Bratkowski, of his daily $3.00 mass stipend, I suppose. Without the sung chants, priests could not take a high mass stipend and would be given only the low mass stipend of $2.00. Interestingly, from the point of view of providence, Bernice and her sisters never took that Alaskan jaunt!

My first trip to St. Dominic's daily mass brought me home to the breakfast table howling with laughter. "You should have seen it," I told my Mom and Dad. "Father Bratkowski wears a dress. Bells ring, folks get up and down and mumble. And Bernice sings in a foreign language. Funniest thing I've ever seen!" My mother, a bridge-playing friend of the organist and a good friend to many Catholics in town, came up with one of her "Just what do you think you're doing?" lines. She told me if I ever made fun of the Catholic mass again I could not go back to learn to substitute for Bernice. Whoops! I began to take the ritual more seriously. Bernice gave me books to read. She also gave me a rosary and told me, "Pray for the gift of faith." I did and the gift was given—in and through the instrumentality of the art of Roman Catholic ritual.

Vatican II, with its many ritual revisions, did not disturb me as it did so many converts of the 1940s and 1950s. I had studied about liturgical reform as a seminarian at St. Bede College in Peru, Illinois, under the mentoring of Father Marion Balsavich, O.S.B., and at St. Paul Seminary in St. Paul, Minnesota, tutored by Father John A. Sweeney. So I was more than ready and willing when "The Changes" began in Advent, 1964, the first year of my ordination to ministerial priesthood. In my home diocese of Peoria, I joined several other dedicated liturgical leaders in helping to give fresh shape to the renewed rites in the first quarter of a century following the council.

For eight years (1979–1987) I served as Director of the Office of Christian Worship and Music in the Diocese of Peoria. It was not any advanced studies in liturgy that gave me the background for such a position. I had done very little specifically in liturgical studies. Nor was it my doctorate in historical theology from Fordham University which "qualified" me for such an appointment by my bishop, Edward R. O'Rourke (who had also given me instructions in the Roman Catholic religion at the Newman Foundation at the University of Illinois back in 1954). It was, rather, my Bachelor of Music degree from the University of Illinois, with an organ performance major, which recommended me for the position—one which I neither sought nor desired at the time. So naturally I tended to think of ritual as a musician does—and so to approach liturgy as an art.

During my years in that office I became increasingly convinced that liturgical reform and renewal was at a major crossroads. The people who worked with liturgy in the parishes of the diocese taught me much about what was still missing in the renewal of worship as well as where we needed to go next. The reform of the structures and texts of the rites were only the first steps. Those were only the tools for liturgy. We had yet to learn how to use them. What we needed to do next, it became clear to me then and is ever more clear now, was to explore anew the very nature of what we do as worshiping assemblies. What do we think we're doing anyway!

What we do is called ritual. That is the form of Roman Catholic liturgical worship. Ritual, by nature, is a whole integrally-woven constellation of patterned repetitive behaviors which review and renew a group's meaning and identity.

It was ritual's beauty which had originally attracted me to the

Roman Catholic Church. But the Vatican II liturgical reform seems to involve a regrettable amnesia about the very nature of our forms of worship. We must recall what it is we do when we call people together in faith to worship. We ask them to participate in rituals.

My conviction is that ritual is an aesthetic form, appealing to the human imagination so that mystery may be experienced as presence in and through the liturgy. It is truly the bodying forth of forms of imagination. As Baron Frederich von Hugel said, liturgy is "the waking up of spirit under the stimulus of sense" (Kenneth Clark, *Civilization,* New York, 1969, p. 50). I have explored the sensual and aesthetic nature of liturgy rather theoretically in an earlier work, *More Than Meets the Eye* (Paulist Press, 1983).

The present book summarizes some of that theory and makes many practical suggestions for aesthetic celebration. It specifically applies artistic insights to the celebration of the eucharist. How would one celebrate ritual aesthetically? And what is clearly a-aesthetic or anti-aesthetic? Those are the two concrete questions underlying this book. It is meant to be a practical book then, detailing how the various parts of the mass can be energized into artistic communal celebrations.

The aesthetic nature of Roman Catholic ritual is affirmed by several prominent writers of this century. Gerardus Van Der Leeuw speaks of liturgy as a work of art which he terms "sacer ludus" (i.e., holy play). It is, he contends, a holy drama which comes closest to perfection. "For whether it is rich or impover-ished, developed or truncated, the liturgy of the Church is in any case drama, and it is in any case art. . . . It is not as though the liturgy represented primarily a work of art. The Church is by no means a dramatic institution. The beauty of the liturgy belongs among the glorious gifts of God which are granted us when we seek the Kingdom of God" (Gerardus Van Der Leeuw, *Sacred and Pro-fane: The Holy in Art.* New York: Holt, Rinehart and Winston, 1963, pp. 80, 93 and 110).

Ralph Adams Cram, the gothic architecture revivalist, also spoke of the liturgy as "a consummate work of art" (Ralph Adams Cram, *My Life in Architecture,* Boston, 1936, p. 234). He wrote that liturgy is the "assembling of all the arts—music, poetry, drama, ceremonial—in one vast organic work of art" and, as such, constitutes humanity's "greatest artistic achievement" (Ralph Adams Cram, "The Artist and the World" in *The Ministry of Art,* Boston, 1914, p. 135). Although my post-Vatican II approach to the art of ritual may differ somewhat from that of Cram in its understanding of ceremonial, the fundamental insight is much the same.

Evelyn Underhill wrote of the aesthetic potential of ritual. It is, she said, "an action and an experience that transcends the logical levels of the mind and demands an artistic rather than an intellectual form of expression." There is always danger, of course, that artistic forms may smother the spirit in worship, *ars gratia artis!* Yet, she was convinced, the aesthetic risk in worship has to be taken because humans are not pure spirits, capable of pure spiritual acts (Evelyn Underhill, *Worship,* New York, 1936, p. 33 and p. 14). She contended that "art in worship is not a mere mutation of the creative work of God; nor is it only a homage rendered to Christ; *by giving embodiment to invisible realities it continues the Incarnation of the Word*" (Underhill, p. 245).

Indeed; the art of ritual makes the holy presence present in and through the embodiment and enactment of aesthetic forms. Albert Hammenstede, understanding liturgy as an art *sui generis* wrote: "All other arts, no matter what their vehicle of expression, do not make present in their forms the realities which they represent. . . . Liturgical art makes present not only an idea but the reality" (cited in Douglass Shand Tucci, "The High Mass As Sacred Dance," *Theology Today,* April, 1977, p. 64).

A more contemporary writer such as Archbishop Rembert G. Weakland, O.S.B., of Milwaukee also emphasizes that liturgy "is a very special kind of experience, one where the aesthetic helps bear the transcendent dimension." In the spring of 1992 Weakland said, "There has always been in our history a deep aesthetic relationship between liturgy and art and that has become an aspect of our Catholic identity and tradition. Perhaps in the United States we have not understood that relationship. We will have trouble with liturgy until we understand its deep aesthetic component. . . ." He contends that the beauty of ritual's aesthetic experience while not faith itself is nevertheless "a kind of instrument or help for the leap of faith" (from "Articulating the Vision," *The Critic,* Spring, 1992, p. 18).

Roman Catholic ritual is not, however, an art of free construction. It is an art grounded in the Roman rite of Vatican II as it is given to the universal church. Artistic ritual in our tradition must be neither novelty nor unlimited creativity. Lest one may think that an aesthetic approach to ritual may not be in accord with the intentions and documents of the official church, I have grounded my observations in the texts of official liturgical documents: *The General Instruction on the Roman Missal, The Constitution on the Sacred Liturgy, Music in Catholic Worship* and *Liturgical Music Today.*

These documents form the skeletal framework for my aesthetic reflections. Only by rooting ourselves in what the church intends can assemblies worship as Roman Catholics. But what the church intends is not just rules and rubrics. It invites us to discover once again the beauty of our tradition of worship, a ritual tradition, an aesthetic tradition.

My original insights about the art of ritual grew out of several weeks which I spent with Dr. David Tracy at the Institute for Ecumenical and Cultural Research at Collegeville, Minnesota during the summer of 1976. In reading under him his fundamental theology work, *Blessed Rage for Order,* the importance of the human imagination in faith—and hence the arts—began to become clear to me. I wish to thank him for originating inspiration and continuing encouragement to pursue the paths of imagination these past fifteen years. A similar expression of gratitude is offered to my colleague in reflection on the imagination, Walter J. Burghardt, S.J., who has, over the years, spurred me on to further work on the imagination as well as offered his supportive and inimitable critique.

Thanks is due to my dear, long-time friend, Sister Audrey Cleary, O.S.B., who carefully and creatively edited the manuscript and made many helpful suggestions. I also thank Douglas Fisher, my editor with Paulist Press, for his encouragement and editorial advice. And, of course, I thank those numberless and unnamed liturgists and musicians with whom I have worked over the years who have helped lead me to these conclusions about the aesthetic nature of liturgy.

May these words inspire liturgists, ministers and worshiping assemblies to conceive, create, compose, choreograph, embody and enact worship as the art it is by its very nature. May this work help us, worshipers all, in the next quarter century to find effective and beautiful forms of imagination which Body Forth the Presence of Mystery!

Part I

1

Where Have We Come From —Liturgically, That Is?

Liturgical renewal within the Roman Catholic Church is truly a long twilight struggle. As with anything living, a mixture of joy and pain is inevitable in growth and development. Like the paschal mystery which the church's liturgy celebrates, worship reform and renewal comes to life only through dying and rising.

Vatican II's *Constitution on the Sacred Liturgy,* promulgated on December 4, 1963, was given birth after years of incubation in the historical research of scholars and in the liturgical practices of several European monasteries, as well as through conciliar labor pains. The first decade of liturgical reform, 1963–1973, was the infancy and childhood period. This was the time of preparation, promulgation and promotion of the new ritual structures and texts. It was carried out in the typically Roman Catholic style of that time, i.e., authoritative, if not authoritarian. Change came by official decree from the top down.

Rome spoke and people jumped, some because they were informed, excited and ready, others because they were simply startled. In many places there was enthusiastic support. From other quarters, silence, even resistance, made the leap forward seem like not much more than a baby step. As one resistant pastor and chair of a diocesan liturgy committee said to me in 1964, the year of my ordination: "We'll say mass in this church facing the people over my dead body. If it's such a good idea to turn the altar around and face the other way, why don't we turn the pews around and let the people look the other way?"

The second decade (1973–1983) of worship renewal, the adolescent phase, followed quite naturally. Official promulgation was followed by local assimilation and adaptation. As the official rites were implemented around the world, they took on more local coloration and parochial flavor. People gradually absorbed the revised rites and adapted them to the needs and styles of their worshiping assemblies. The genus of the renewed Roman rite was becoming somewhat varied in its species. Inculturation was underway—in a way!

This brought an interesting reversal of energies. Liturgical renewal began to originate more from the bottom. Grassroots experience with the new rites gave rise to many new questions about the reform, questions about both structures and texts. These were questions born not of scholarship, not of rarified monastic practice, and not of conciliar politics. The new questions grew within the vital womb of ecclesial experience, the living worship of internationally diverse faith communities. To put it simply, and not without some humor, the question of the second decade was: How is the Roman rite playing in Peoria?

Both continuity and discontinuity were created during these two earliest decades of post-conciliar liturgical renewal. Praying assemblies began to make the revised rites their own. To do this they began to make adaptations which they judged useful for smoother, more organic communal prayer. Some of these experiments were wise and legal. Others were neither. But in the process something was learned, namely, the value of exploring and questioning *the liturgical experience itself.* As Rembert Weakland told liturgists in the mid-1960s, the underlying question for liturgical renewal must become: What is the liturgical experience *supposed* to be?

While the first decade has found many opposed and some in favor of the new liturgy, and while most, if truth were told, were probably neutral, the second decade saw a growing number accepting and even liking "The Changes." Through extensive explanations from the pulpit, classroom and printed matter, through some ritual refinements and, more importantly, through some prayerful experiences with the revised rites, most folks, by the early 1980s, had come to accept "The Changes."

"THE CHANGES"

What were the more noticeable changes? First and foremost the ritual structures and texts were changed. Both were simplified. Texts were created in the vernacular, the language of the people, rather than the age-old Latin. Duplications of texts and ritual gestures were eliminated. The rites were "drawn up so that they express more clearly the holy things which they signify."

This was done so that "the Christian people, so far as possible, should be enabled to understand them with ease and to take part in them fully, actively, and as befits a community" (*Constitution on the Sacred Liturgy* [Hereafter CSL], #21). Further, "these rites should be distinguished by a noble simplicity; they should be short, clear, and unencumbered by useless repetitions; they should be within the people's powers of comprehension, and normally should not require much explanation" (CSL #34).

Second, the major change experienced by the assembly was the expansion of liturgical ministries beyond the ordained to the laity. Due to a longstanding clerically-focused celebration of the mass, and due also to the liturgical requirement of the Latin language, the community's participation had been either quite passive (following the priest's words and gestures) or semi-active in Latin dialogue masses and in singing "at mass." After the council, however, *everyone* was invited to celebrate the liturgy, not just an active priest watched by a passive people. Even the ways in which the clergy were to lead within the ritual changed.

According to the *General Instruction of the Roman Missal:* "All in the assembly gathered for mass have an individual right and duty to contribute their participation in ways differing according to the diversity of their order and liturgical function. Thus in carrying out this function, all, whether ministers or laypersons, should do all and only those parts that belong to them, so that the very arrangement of the celebration itself makes the church stand out as being formed in a structure of different orders and ministries" (G.I. #58).

Third, there was a distinct difference in the variety of ministers serving within the mass. Members of the assembly were invited to come forward to serve as liturgical ministers. There were acolytes, lectors, commentators, music ministers, ushers (now often called ministers of hospitality) and extraordinary ministers of eucharist. Their function was to serve the assembly's worship and to evoke from the assembly a greater degree of active participation in the liturgy. In their preparation for these ministries, they were informed of three fundamental requirements for every minister: understanding, techniques and faith-filled, prayerful presence.

THREE REQUIREMENTS FOR LITURGICAL MINISTRY

Let us examine the three requirements in some detail.

First, *understanding*. One who ministers in worship should know the *what* and the *why* of the liturgy in order to serve intelligently and prayerfully. This involves a basic theological comprehension of the nature of Roman Catholic worship as well as more specific knowledge about the role in which one is to serve.

Second, *techniques*. Since knowledge alone does not a good liturgical minister make, one must also learn *how* to function in his or her special ministry. Let us examine both the official description of these roles and also some of the interior and exterior changes which "The Changes" called for in the ministers' self-awareness and ritual behavior.

Priests. Since altars began to be turned so that the priests and ministers faced the assembly, priests were made aware that their body language speaks perhaps louder than their words. They had to learn the movements, postures and facial expressions which were both truly natural to each individual yet appropriate within the formal, ritual context. They discovered that facing the congregation is only the first step in energizing an assembly toward communal ritual behavior. What one's face, indeed, what one's whole body, "says" is the next step. Ritual is the art of the body. As Ralph Adams Cram said, "the controlled movements of the body" must be learned like any other art—by rehearsal.

John Henry Newman spoke of "the sacred dance of the ministers." "If they are to invoke within themselves what it is their duty to invoke in everyone else, the ministers and their attendants must act, dance, or whatever. The sacred dance, like all liturgical art, must struggle for incarnation in it of the supernatural if it is to be transfigured" (Tucci, pp. 68–69).

Some clerics, however, continued to "say mass" just as they did when they faced the sanctuary wall. The body was turned around but the people could well have been behind the priest or completely absent, for little notice was paid to them by the presider. Mass still looked quite private even though it was being "said" or "read" in public. One prominent cardinal, John Cody, the Archbishop of Chicago, read the entire eucharistic prayer at the 1971 ordination of Edward W. O'Rourke as Bishop of Peoria with his immense body "versus populum," but with his head turned forever sideways toward the sacramentary, never looking at the assembly. He did not appear to know even the words of institution, so glued were his eyes to the book. Custody of the eyes, assiduously taught in the seminaries of yesteryear, did not serve celebrants well in the new liturgy. Celibates found their very bodies—indeed, their persons—exposed in ways that would, in time, bring far more changes into the life of the church than mere ritual reforms.

Deacons. The permanent diaconate, restored by Vatican II, called both married and single men into ordained ministry alongside transitional deacons preparing for priesthood. Among the ministers, according to the General Instruction and ancient tradition, deacons have "first place." Although their ordination places them outside the lay state canonically and theologically, their lives remain very much lay in character. In the liturgy, the deacon "proclaims the gospel, sometimes preaches God's word, leads the general intercessions, assists the priest, gives communion to the people (in particular, ministering the chalice), and sometimes gives directions regarding the assembly's moving, standing, kneeling, or sitting" (G.I. # 61).

Just as priests must learn to function facing the people, so deacons should be prepared for a very *visible* liturgical presence and role—not just heard in words but fully seen in human embodiment. They need to learn how to live and move and have their being as ritual persons. From the way they wear their vestments to the way they process, from their prayerful attention to all that is happening during the ritual to their faith-filled proclamation of the gospel, from their assistance at the altar to the dismissal of the assembly, deacons are ritual performers—actors, artists of ritual.

An incident recounted in my earlier book *More Than Meets the Eye*, (Paulist Press, 1983) bears retelling in this context for priests and deacons, indeed, for all liturgical ministers.

The scene: a priest of middle age is simulating a eucharistic liturgy for a university drama professor in order to improve his celebrating style. The priest is at an "altar," facing the professor. He begins to recite the preface of the eucharistic prayer, only to discover that he is not on the right page of the sacramentary. He begins the preface dialogue anyway, since he knows the words: "The Lord be with you," etc., while leafing through the book, eyes searching the pages for the proper place.

The drama professor interrupted: "Wait a minute, Father. What are you doing?"

"Well, I'm reading what's prescribed here in the book—'The Lord be with you' . . . 'Lift up your hearts,' " replied the priest.

"But don't you realize," the dramatist said, "this is a dialogue? You should be looking at the people."

So the priest looked straight ahead and said with neither facial expression nor verbal inflection, "The Lord be with you," etc.

"Wait a minute, Father. What are you doing now?" repeated the artist.

Now the priest became annoyed at the interruption. With frustration evident in his voice, he shot back, "I'm looking at the people just the way you told me to do."

"But doesn't this mean anything to you? Don't you have any feelings when you greet your people? Couldn't you put some expression into your face, your sounds, your body language?"

"Look," said the priest with restrained anger, "I'm a priest, not an actor."

The dramatist retorted, "Well, Father, if you don't want to be an actor, take off the costume!"

Liturgical ministers are indeed actors in the drama called ritual. It is not *Hamlet* of course. But the organization of ritual energies are meant to resemble more the events of the stage than static, communal recipe-reading experiences.

Lectors "proclaim the readings from scripture, with the exception of the gospel. . . . Those who exercise the ministry of reader . . . must be truly qualified and carefully prepared in order that the faithful will develop a warm and lively love for scripture from listening to the reading of the sacred texts" (G.I. #66). Lectors were often the first new ministers to serve when the changes began. While it was assumed that this ministry would be an easy one for lay entry since after all *everyone can read,* it soon became apparent that not everyone *can* read, at least not in public.

Proclaiming the word, it was soon discovered, is itself an art which requires far more than the simple ability to speak words. Public reading calls for a rhythm in pacing, both with the words and the spatial acoustics. Other requirements include: proper use of a microphone, ease of eye contact with the assembly and consistent use of the proper lectionary rather than a throwaway missalette. Even more importantly, scriptural proclamation needs to become not just words, even well-spoken words. It must be a proclamation of faith. Lectors are to share the faith which belongs not only to the church, but which is also being personally appropriated by each lector.

Liturgical musicians—choir and directors, organists, cantors, song leaders and other instrumentalists—play a dual role. They support the assembly's singing and they add their own unique beauty and solemnity to the liturgy (G.I. #63 and 64). They energize the assembly to become a performing audience at prayer. Many musicians had to learn to perform not just *for* an assembly but *with* the assembly as the people began to take a more active musical part in the rites.

Song leaders and cantors are important. The song leader energizes the assembly's song. The cantor sings the biblical song between the readings. The essential importance of a fine organ and experienced organist is obvious. This is leading parishes to purchase better organs and, at long last, to provide a more adequate budget line for hiring and/or training parish organists. Other musical instruments have been introduced, such as guitars, and wind and percussion instruments. Styles of music for worship have changed, too, as contemporary and secular kinds of songs are employed, baptized into sacred usage.

Extraordinary ministers of eucharist are commissioned to share in the distribution of communion. These new ministers also greatly facilitate the expanding practice of communion under both kinds. Since this entails a more complicated communion procession, we are coming to realize more than ever that smooth liturgy involves choreography as well as planning-on-paper.

Commentators were helpful in the early phase of renewal to explain the meaning of the new rites. In commentaries "meticulously prepared and marked by a simple brevity" (G.I. #68a), they helped introduce people to fuller comprehension and participation. However, as people have become better informed and experienced in the new rites, commentators have proved superfluous, indeed, intrusive in the rituals except, perhaps, for special occasions and liturgies with which the assemblies are not familiar.

Ushers, one of the most ancient lay ministries in liturgy, are encouraged to think of themselves as more than passing-out-picking-up, money-taking, seat-giving agents (G.I. # 68b and c). Women are joining men in this role. They are being called now by the descriptive title of greeters or ministers of hospitality. Their warm welcome begins the energy of hospitality that should characterize the entire celebration.

Finally, *acolytes* serve at the altar, assisting the priest and deacon in preparing the altar and the vessels (G.I. #65). These persons who, prior to Vatican II, spoke the mass responses in the name of and in place of the people, are now invited to sing and pray together with the assembly as well as perform their practical duties with cross, responses, wine, water, bell, book and candles. It may be that such an expanded role for the acolyte calls for more than small boys serving in this ministry. They are perhaps the least likely to be prepared for all the role entails now that serving mass is supposed to be much more than a training camp for young prospective male seminarians!

To reiterate: all of these liturgical ministers need both an *understanding* of liturgy and *training* in the techniques of their offices. But most importantly they require an ever deepening interior life of *faith* which expresses itself in *prayerful presence.* And the greatest of these gifts is faith! We all know what a difference it makes in our ministries if what we are saying, singing or doing flows from our personal relationship to the Lord and to God's people. Most in the assembly are aware if the ministers are merely doing a job or are celebrating their faith. Ministers are more likely to be instruments of grace in transforming others if they themselves are being changed by word and sacrament. Ministry, then, is not only *what we do* or *how we do it.* Most importantly it is *who we are becoming* in Christ Jesus.

While the first two decades of reform and renewal brought forth new rites, spaces and ministries, the third decade calls for even deeper change in ministers and assemblies. Liturgical renewal was never primarily about turning altars around. It has not been principally about getting laity into liturgical ministries. The new ritual's focus is not actually on the folks "up front" at all. Renewal of rites is primarily about *turning people around*—turning toward God by turning toward one another and also turning toward the inner reaches of oneself.

It has become increasingly clear that the great and continuing task of liturgical renewal is that of forming the primary ministers of the liturgy, the worshipers themselves, the assembly. As this role of the assembly is explored and developed, we would do well to listen to what assemblies are saying about their experiences with the post-conciliar liturgies for the past nearly thirty years.

2

What's Missing? The Mystery! Why Is Mystery Missing?

Despite the obvious improvements in the post-conciliar liturgy, a significant number of worshipers have noticed something missing. Many call it "the sense of the sacred." What seems missing is mystery—the awe, the holiness and wonder which had been the liturgical experience of Roman Catholics prior to Vatican II. With the priest now facing the folks and the people participating together in the vernacular, some persons-in-the-pews are finding mass not much different from ordinary life. The otherness seems absent. With so much verbal participation and direct understanding of the words, something of transcendence, the experience of incomprehensible and ineffable mystery has been diminished or, in some cases, even disappeared.

While some post-conciliar theologians said that the sacred had to be *discovered* in the secular, the sacred at mass seemed for many to have been *replaced* by the secular. Both nostalgia buffs as well as scholars and ordinary parishioners sensed this. Without wishing to eliminate the principal values upon which the reform had been based, a cry has arisen for the retrieval of the sense of the sacred in worship.

Active participation has indeed made more people busy doing more things. But has it more effectively created the conditions of possibility for people to express and experience the sacred? External participation is meant to deepen and enrich interior participation, not to eliminate it. Yet many have been saying for some time: "How can we experience the presence of God, the Holy One, in this new, active, indeed sometimes overly busy liturgy?"

Delegates to the 1985 Extraordinary Synod of Bishops in Rome surfaced similar concerns. While the 165 heads of National Bishops' Conferences agreed that liturgical renewal is the most visible fruit of the whole work of the council, they pointed out that one of the most pressing problems with liturgical renewal is the diminished sense of the sacred.

At that synod, Augustin Cardinal Mayer of the Vatican's Congregation for Divine Worship, stated that the intentions of the council will not be fully implemented if a proper sense of mystery is not cultivated in liturgical celebration. "There are signs that such a dimension to liturgical celebration is actively desired and sought by many of the faithful, and this aspiration should be met by the mode of celebration. . . . The element of adoration, praise and thanksgiving should be promoted as pertaining to the primary end of liturgical action" (press reports of the Extraordinary Synod of Bishops, Vatican Press Office).

A good number of both progressives and conservatives agree about this concern. Notre Dame liturgist, Mark Searle, commenting on the Notre Dame Study of Catholic Parish Life, writes: ". . . the overall impression created by the liturgies we observed was one of mechanical and listless performance. Rarely was there an atmosphere of deeply prayerful involvement. . . . There is little evidence of ceremony and ritual splendor. . . . The impression was one of ritual minimalism . . . and the continuing victory of pragmatism over symbolism. . . . The opportunities offered by the rite for solemnizing the liturgy are not much used in this country" (*Worship,* July, 1986, pp. 317 and 319).

Joseph Cardinal Ratzinger wrote just prior to the synod: "One shudders at the lackluster face of the post-conciliar liturgy as it has become, or one is simply bored with its hankering after banality and its lack of artistic standards." According to him, "what needs to be discovered in an entirely new way is the 'given, nonarbitrary, constant and unshakeable character of liturgical worship.' " Ratzinger, too, noted the need for mystery to be experienced by worshipers. "Nowadays the really widespread demand is not for a secularized liturgy but, on the contrary, for a new encounter with the sacred through a worship that manifests the presence of the Eternal" (Joseph Cardinal Ratzinger with Vittorio Messori, *The Ratzinger Re-*

port, Herefordshire, England: Fowler Wright Books Limited, 1985, pp. 121 and 125–126 and 131).

The Extraordinary Synod expressed hope for a retrieval of the sense of mystery in liturgy. In its final report, the bishops at the synod noted that, in spite of secularism, there are signs of a return to the sacred, a new hunger for the transcendent and divine. "To cooperate with this return to the sacred and to defeat secularism, we must open the way to the dimension of the 'divine' or of mystery, and offer approaches of faith to the people of our time" (Final Report, Extraordinary Synod of Bishops, December, 1985). This retrieval involves probing the meaning of "the mode of the celebration" mentioned by Mayer, the "victory over pragmatism" and ritual minimalism noted by Searles, and the loss of the aesthetic lamented by Ratzinger.

THE MEANING OF MYSTERY

At this juncture one must ask: What is "the sense of the sacred"? Surely it is neither the mysteriousness effected by yesteryear's smells and bells, nor is it the privatized, distancing provided by the Latin language and Gregorian chants sung only by a choir, nor does it call for the elimination of communication and comprehension by the assembly—all of which characterized pre-conciliar liturgical experience. Retrieving mystery does not mean engendering certain predetermined feelings of awe, mystery and good fellowship. All of that may be "mysterious" to the old or "awesome" to the young and that may be what some nostalgia buffs of all ages long for. But that is not the authentic sense of the sacred.

Experienced mystery is the felt consciousness within participants that they are being grasped by a reality greater than and, indeed, beyond themselves, both individually and collectively. To call liturgy a "celebration," as has been done since Vatican II, is not to equate it with a birthday party. It is not merely another coming together of folks like life's other gatherings. The worshiping assembly makes present the mystical body of Christ in which mystery is experienced as presence, the Spirit within each one and within the assembly as a whole. As St. Paul wrote: "The Mystery is Christ in you." Without this sense of God's otherness made present in ritual, "God is simply the self magnified," according to Robert Bellah (Robert Bellah, et al., *Habits of the Heart*, New York: Harper and Row, 1985, p. 235).

What distinguishes the liturgy from other human activities, according to Roman Catholic tradition, is this directly symbolized expression and experience of mystery. As the *Constitution on the Liturgy*, #2, states: "The liturgy . . . is the outstanding means whereby the faithful may express in their lives, and manifest to others, the mystery of Christ and the real nature of the church." As *Environment and Art in Catholic Worship*, #12 and 18, point out: "The experience of mystery which liturgy offers is found in its God-consciousness and God-centeredness." "An important part of contemporary church renewal is the awareness of the community's recognition of the sacred."

The holy, according to Rudolf Otto, is felt at once as objective. It is a reality more than the self to which individuals respond interiorly. "It is the emotion of a creature, submerged and overwhelmed by its own nothingness in contrast to that which is supreme above all creatures. . . . It must be experienced as present. . . . And the proper response to that presence is adoration, awe, wonder, humility and reverence" (Rudolf Otto, *The Idea of the Holy*, London: Oxford University Press, 1923, pp. 10–11). This is what is meant by those who say the mystery is missing in mass: The experience of the presence of the holy and the appropriate personal and communal response of praise and thanksgiving.

3

The Reasons for the Problem

Two fundamental reasons can be offered for the diminishment of the sense of the sacred in the liturgy. One is cultural and the other is ecclesial.

THE CULTURAL PROBLEM

First, contemporary western culture is suffused with secularism. Consequently, persons living in such a society find "the sacred" a difficult concept to grasp and an elusive reality to experience. Secularism's autonomic worldview, namely, what you see is all there is, prescinds from the dimension of mystery in all creation. In a world where what meets the eye is all that counts, more-than-meets-the-eye, like the holy, is readily discounted.

Our culture, while teaching the *facts* of science and the products of technology, often neglects the human *meaning* of these advances. The arts, which can be avenues into life's spirit and meaning, are either not stressed or are eliminated in academic institutions which principally promote careerism, production as an end in itself, and financial profit as the bottom line. An education which relies primarily upon analytic and discursive reason greatly reduces the possibility and the extent of human knowing. Without the arts as the expression of imagination, teachers may dispense facts without human meaning and share information without human insight.

What is truly human in reality cannot be simply *pointed to* but can be *embodied* in the shapes, patterns and forms of the arts. A retrieval of the arts in the academic and societal enterprise is a major factor in educating beyond the superficial, in leading people out into the deep streams of human living. John Dewey states categorically: "The final measure of the quality of that culture is the arts which flourish. Compared with their influence things directly taught by word and precept are pale and ineffectual" (John Dewey, *Art As Experience,* New York: Minton, Balch & Co., p. 345).

Living is an art in itself. The quality of life resembles the aesthetic qualities in works of art. "The relation between the qualities of the art work and the qualities of human experience is felt by the perceiver of the work as 'significance.' " Dewey warns that a culture which separates art from life separates the person from life's fullness, from participating and helping to create life's meaning. "Instruction in the arts of life is something other than conveying information about them. It is a matter of communication and participation in values of life by means of the imagination, and works of art are the most intimate and energetic means of aiding individuals to share in the arts of living" (Dewey, p. 336).

Imprisoned by the cult of materialism and captured by consumerism, our culture is caught in a crisis beyond imagination precisely because it denigrates the arts as creations of the imagination. As Archibald MacLeish has written: "The crisis of our time . . . is not a crisis of the hands but of the heart . . . a failure of the spirit to imagine and desire" (Archibald MacLeish, *Listen to Love,* N.Y.: Regina Press, 1969, p. 208).

Robert Shaw, the virtuoso conductor and musical artist, has expressed his concern about the disappearing "conservative arts" as strongly and artistically as anyone I know. The arts, he holds, "in-form" humans. Through the "making" that is the arts, we are inwardly formed to find our "is-ness" and our "relation to others." Shaw continues: "I suspect that in the long run—if there is a long run—the arts will be seen to be the lode-star of Man's humanity—even more than religious or political structures. . . .

"In the first place, it is clear that a commitment to the creative process starts the human animal on an endless, thorny and lonesome road of self-discovery, away from the comforts, blurred objectives and compromises of institutions. . . .

"In the second place, the arts are concerned not with the consumption, sale or other exploitation of earth's material wonders—not even with their recycling—but with their reincarnation. They propose not a mounting monopoly of a medium of exchange, but the sweet, quiet exchange of truth and beauty. . . .

"And in the third place, in a time and a society whose values are geared to the biggest, the fastest and mostest, whose gaze is fixed desperately upon the future—as far at least as the next election or life after death or prosperity, whichever should happen to come first—the arts offer an historical perspective. For their concern is with originality—meaning, that which has origins. Thus the arts lead man to consider and build upon his own beginnings—his essence and his potential. . . .

"For finally, the simple truth is that every man is an artist—whether he wants it or not.

"The only question is whether he's enough of an artist to fulfill his humanity—and to fill full his short mortality.

"The understandings of the spirit are not easily come by. It takes a creative mind to respond to a creator's mind. It takes a holy spirit to receive the Holy Spirit. And "just as I am" is not nearly good enough.

"There's no easy-on-easy-off for Truth. There's no landscaped approach to beauty.

"You scratch and scramble around intellectual granites; you try to defuse or tether your emotional tantrums; you pray for the day when your intellect and your instinct can co-exist, that the brain need not calcify the heart, nor the heart o'er flood and drown all reason.

"But in the struggle lies dignity and a tolerable destiny. (The alternatives to life aren't all that attractive anyway.)

"So while we're here, let's hold fast to the liberating, conserving arts. For man in his available glory is clothed only by such as these.

"And without them there soon could be no body to clothe" (unpublished address, "The Conservative Arts" given to the author by Robert Shaw).

The dimunition or elimination of the arts in this country creates problems for the art of living and for the art of ritual as well. Both a predominantly secular worldview and these cultural failures in aesthetics dramatically affect Catholics' current understanding of and participation in liturgy.

When a culture becomes as secular and a-aesthetic or anti-aesthetic as our own, worship can be reduced to just another purely human expression. It becomes only what *we* do. Such horizontal reductionism is not the authentic ritual tradition of Roman Catholicism. Liturgy is, first and foremost, the action of Jesus Christ and *then* of his body, the church. It ". . . does not come from what *we do* but from the fact that something is *taking place* here that all of us together cannot 'make.' In the liturgy there is a power, an energy at work which not even the Church as a whole can generate: what it manifests is the wholly other, coming to us through community. . ." (*The Ratzinger Report, op.cit.,* p. 126).

THE ECCLESIAL PROBLEM

Second, the ecclesial part of the problem needs exploration. The church's liturgical reform, in its early stages, was founded largely upon the extensive research of scholars but not sufficiently upon the experience of worshipers nor upon an aesthetic appreciation of the very nature of ritual action. Liturgical scholars gave the church new ritual structures and texts. However, they were unable to provide the tools to transform the rites into celebrative events of mystery. But then scholars *qua* scholars are not necessarily the ones with the practical skills needed to lift liturgy off the page into genuine celebrations of faith.

The foundations which were well-laid by scholarship led to three permanently valid and valuable principles which undergirded and guided the initial reform of the rites. Paradoxically, these principles, not adequately grasped in the broadest implications, also became the source of the current problems in ongoing worship renewal. Those three principles expressed in the *Constitution on the Sacred Liturgy* are: 1) active participation; 2) communication; and 3) comprehension.

First, *active participation*. Liturgy is meant to be more than the actions of priest, choir and acolytes. Therefore, worship had to become more truly the "full, active and conscious" act of everyone present if the nature of the church was to be expressed and experienced, as well as the mystery of Christ.

The second value guiding the reform was *communication*. For this to come about, forms of expression were chosen to facilitate communication among the members of the assembly. The language of the people was incorporated so that worshipers could interact in word and song. With this increased ritual communication, hospitality became a heightened value. Now the value of reverence which had so characterized pre-conciliar liturgy had to be balanced with the value of hospitality. Forms of ritual expression were called for, therefore, which engaged the participants with one another and with God-among us, as well as with the God who lives within and exists above.

The third guiding value was *comprehension.* If all were to participate and communicate, they had to understand what was happening and what was being said. Latin and Gregorian chants, venerable vehicles that they were and still are, were considered inadequate to express the mystery in such a way that participants could understand what was going on. Therefore, words in the vernacular began to bear most of the expressive weight in implementing the three critical values which guided liturgical reform: participation, communication and comprehension.

With such emphasis being placed upon words—those rational, discursive forms of expression—and upon external activities at mass, people began to experience the loss of the sense of mystery. The liturgy was becoming word-heavy, logical, didactic and explanatory. The true symbolic beauty of the Roman rite became bogged down with wordiness and busyness. From the excessive interpolations by the presiders to the canned remarks of commentators, from the redundant summaries of the scriptures by the lectors to the insipid greetings by the song leaders, the liturgy was becoming a highly didactic experience, one which engaged discursive reason through conceptual and verbal symbols. Explanations replaced explorations. Instead of symbolic action engaged in by the entire assembly, ritual was expressed in such fashion that it was too often experienced as communal recipe-reading, not just by the priest and acolytes but now by the whole verbalizing assembly.

The three values of active participation, communication and comprehension which guided the first stages of liturgical reform, although remaining valid, seem to have led us down some dead-end trails. Early on and even now in many instances, *active partici-*

pation seemed to mean getting more people busy doing more things. But isn't external participation fundamentally aimed toward interior awareness of God's transforming presence and action? Isn't the exterior ritual action principally for the sake of an interior deepening awareness of God's Spirit acting through the assembly's enactment of word and sacrament? *Communication* in ritual tended to become more a kind of "folksy clubiness" than communing with the Godhead in and through assembling with other believers for communal prayer. *Comprehension* is essential of course. However, it must not be forgotten that, ultimately in ritual, persons are relating to the incomprehensible mystery of God. To try to put too much into words within the ritual is to lessen or lose the experience of mystery which ritual expresses.

For some years after worship renewal began, well-intentioned catechists recognized that something was missing in our early efforts. Because of their direct pastoral contacts, they felt called to rush into the liturgical gap in order to bring fresh life to the new but apparently ineffective rites. With great good will and enthusiasm, but sometimes with less than an adequate understanding of symbolic expression, they took over the obviously necessary task of making the new liturgy more understandable and more vital.

Religious educators as liturgists did indeed involve more people doing more things, relevant and experiential things, but it was through things primarily expressed verbally. Often this led even more deeply into the liturgical trap of wordiness: too many explanations of what symbols "as things" mean; too many didactic songs which did not necessarily fit the rhythm of the ritual; and too much novelty passed off as creativity. Creative ritual was surely needed but it was not to be accomplished through improvised novelty. Today similar problems arise when catechists without the insights of ritual artists shape liturgical aspects of the Rite of Christian Initiation of Adults. Rituals can become too busy, lacking in simple symbolical power and overly-expository.

Scholars, many of whom have been astute liturgical historians rather than adept practitioners of ritual art, also sense that there is a serious problem with the reform. Some blame the revised yet still cluttered ritual structures which, in some instances, reflect more political compromise than flowing ritual. Others find the flaws to be

in the translations of the prosaic vernacular texts. Still others criti-
cize the liturgical ministers for their lack of preparation, skill, and
understanding. Some find fault with the space in which liturgy is
enacted since older church architecture tended to organize the worship area more like a theater for passive viewing than an arena for
gathering believers around an ambo and an altar. Still others, reflecting from the perspective of the social sciences, complain that the
culture is antithetical to good ritual. Undoubtedly, each analysis of
the problem yields a useful and correct, albeit partial, insight into
the difficulties with ritual reform. However, even if all of the above
problems were adequately addressed, the problem of lifting ritual
off the page into an energized celebration would remain because,
ultimately, the ritual problem is one of effective performance.

As Catholics—scholars, liturgists and persons-in-the-pew—
have reveled in being allowed to use our own language in liturgy
and in grounding the renewed rites more thoroughly in our past
traditions, a fundamental fact about the languages and forms of
ritual has been overlooked. Liturgy is symbolic action, specified by
words not the other way around. Words cannot be the primary
forms of expression in ritual. They are inadequate means to express and create the conditions of possibility for experiencing the
incomprehensible mystery of Christ. Words address and engage
discursive reason. They create *explanations about* the Holy One.
They are not the best ways to open believers to an *exploration of*
the presence of the sacred either in worship or in life.

4

An Approach to a Solution: Understanding Ritual as an Art

Three decades of worship reform have led toward a retrieval of those forms of expression most appropriate for liturgy. The forms of expression best suited to bring about an experience of the mystery of Christ and the church are images, symbols, myths and ritual actions. These are languages of liturgy which are meant to engage the mind imagining rather than the mind thinking. These languages engage the human imaginative system in such a way that active participants can be opened to experience presence, mystery, God-with-us, God-within-us.

Since images, symbols, myths and ritual actions are the proper forms of expression for ritual, then worship, as an expressive form, is best understood as an aesthetic form because these are properly aesthetic modes of expression. These ritual "languages" can open the imagination to an awareness of and an experience of the presence of mystery through an engagement of the imagination. Ritual is, therefore, an art. Rituals are not just structures and texts to be read. Rituals are a species of drama. Rituals must be *enacted and embodied.*

Herein, I submit, lies a fundamental problem with post-conciliar worship reform and renewal. It is a problem which liturgical scholars and worship practitioners have only begun to grasp and face. Liturgy has not been approached as drama, as an art. It has not been sufficiently understood as aesthetic in its human, expressive core. Does this not speak to Mayer's question about "the mode of the celebration"? Could this be what Ratzinger meant when he said that "the liturgy has lost its artistic standards"?

Isn't this the "victory of pragmatism over symbolism" and "ritual minimalism" mentioned by Searle?

Ritual is a performing art. As such it resembles drama, dance, music and poetry. Like drama, ritual enacts a story. It plays out the continuing saga of God's dealings with people which includes past, present and future dimensions. Like music, ritual has innate rhythms. Each moment prepares for the next and each element flows out of what precedes. Again, like music, ritual involves the building of tensions and resolutions through the use of sounds and silence which create an aural experience of passage. Like dance, ritual involves movement becoming gesture, i.e., movement with symbolic meaning, such as processions, upraised hands, the laying on of hands, and eating and drinking. Like poetry, ritual uses words, not for explanation and communicating knowledge, but for exploration and creating insight into truth with "feelingfulness," to borrow a word from Susanne Langer's book on aesthetic philosophy, *Feeling and Form* (Susanne Langer, *Feeling and Form,* N.Y.: Charles Scribner's Sons, 1953).

If it is important to understand that ritual's proper "mode of celebration" is aesthetic, it is equally important to stress that ritual is not merely a *hybrid* of these four performing arts. One should not speak of liturgy *and* the arts. Liturgy does not *use* the arts in order to become aesthetic. *Liturgy is an integral aesthetic form in itself.* It resembles other arts but it must become its own integral art form. To do so, it has to take other art forms into itself much in the way a poem becomes a song when set to music. The words of a song are no longer merely a poem. They have been transformed into music. Music is the commanding, overarching aesthetic form which binds words and music together. The art of poetry has been subsumed into the art of music. The same transformation of art forms must take place when any art is integrated into the art of ritual. Liturgy uses dramatic action, meaningful gesture, musical sound and silence, and poetic expression. But these art forms must lose themselves as they become elements of another commanding art form, namely, ritual art. All elements "compenetrate" in aesthetic ritual. The action stalls "when its parts are not smoothly integrated" (Tucci, p. 70).

This aesthetic approach to liturgy has at least one potential danger. It could make ritual once again merely a performance by the ministers for a passive assembly. If that were to happen, it would be pre-Vatican II worship revisited with isolated individuals attempting to act like a community. To avoid making the assembly even more inactive than it even now regrettably is, ritual must be conceived, created, composed and choreographed as *an art of a performing audience.* The artists of ritual are not the folks up front, the multiple ministers. The artists are none other than all of the members of the assembly, including ministers. "Ritual as art must not be done *for* but rather *with* the assembly which is, in a very real sense, a *community* of believers, not merely isolated individuals" (Patrick Collins, *More Than Meets the Eye,* New York: Paulist Press, 1983, p. 128).

HOW DOES RITUAL ART LOOK, SOUND AND FEEL

Aesthetic ritual relies heavily upon what is seen, heard and felt. In a sense, what people see is what they get. In the liturgy, faith is embodied and enacted, continuing the sacramental principle of the incarnation. The liturgy effects what it signifies. In other words, it works through the symbolic actions in which the Spirit is present. Analogously, just as Jesus could be called "the Art of God Incarnate" (Aidan Nichols, *The Art of God Incarnate,* New York: Paulist Press, 1980), so the church, particularly in its liturgical celebrations, incarnates and makes symbolically present participatory presence/mystery.

What, then, moves ritual beyond structures and texts toward an aesthetic experience? Perhaps that question may be best addressed by pointing not only to what makes it aesthetic in sight, sound and feeling but by describing what constitutes anti-aesthetic ritual as well.

In regard to *sight,* ministers' sensitivity to the way their bodies are clothed and move can make processions become significant gestures symbolizing going up to the house of the Lord rather than simply resembling pragmatic movements from here to there. Processions are a form of dance—movement transformed into gesture. John Henry Newman spoke of "the sacred dance of the ministers" (Tucci, *op. cit.,* p. 68). Ritual processions may be described as a middle ground between dance and drill.

Priests robed in tacky vestments, looking like unmade beds, and moving without any sense of dramatic bearing, are anti-aesthetic. Acolytes carrying cross and candles in a crooked fashion and at varied levels, or processing with uneven spaces between them act in an anti-aesthetic fashion. Processing ministers who do not sing, who waddle up the aisle swinging their arms or who carry the book of the gospels or lectionary under their arms are anti-aesthetic. Ministers who arrive in the sanctuary wandering around, apparently not knowing where to go next and without any sense of the choreographics of the procession's termination are anti-aesthetic.

In regard to *sound,* ministers who serve aesthetically must choose words carefully and truthfully, even poetically. When it comes to words in ritual, less is most often more. Presiders who, after the conclusion of the processional hymn, say "Let us *begin* our prayer, in the name of the Father . . ." are telling a ritual lie. They contribute to anti-aestheticism by words which indicate they are unaware that the ritual already began before the priest opened his mouth. Lectors who use throwaway words such as: "Our first reading is a reading from , , ." are anti-aesthetic. Such language is redundant, more explanatory than proclamatory. There is no need to number the readings or to use the word "reading" twice. Musicians who rush into the responsorial psalm without any appropriate reflective silence following the preceding scripture are anti-aesthetic. The rhythms of sound and silence between the various parts of the liturgy help to make ritual more than a recited recipe.

In regard to the *feeling tone* of the liturgical experience, ministers appropriately take their own feelingful energies from what preceded their own actions and words. The actual, virtual feelings felt and projected by the ministers flow from the interrelationship of the parts of the ritual as well as the interactions between the ministers. Ministers who do not interact with one another, but rather await their turn to do their independent parts are anti-aesthetic. True dramatic-ritual interaction is essential to aesthetic flow. What happens just before one minister's part sets up what is to follow. Picking up on the preceding tempo, tone, rhythm is what can liberate the inner rhythms of the ritual as well as the prayerful imaginations of the participants. Ushers who mechanically "pass out and pick up" without warmly welcoming members of the assembly are anti-aesthetic. Ministers of hospitality can energize the assembly into their own hospitality and reverence, thus helping to create the "mode of the celebration." Assembly members who either never pick up a hymnal or who perpetually bury their heads in missalettes are anti-aesthetic. Worshipers who never reach out to others in the assembly at the greeting of peace, or who constantly gawk around during the ritual are anti-aesthetic. As stated above, the greatest challenge in liturgical renewal involves forming the assembly in the art of liturgical prayer. Assemblies of worshipers are still struggling to appropriate, interiorize and more fully appreciate the post-conciliar reformed and renewed forms of communal ritual prayer. There are miles to go before assemblies learn the fullest sense of celebrating prayerful rituals which are both communal and, at the same time, personal, yet never merely private.

WHERE ARE WE GOING—AESTHETICALLY, THAT IS?

After nearly thirty years of official liturgical reform and renewal, the church has at its disposal the structural and textual products of scholars. It also has the post-conciliar experiences of worshiping communities. Surely no one has all of the answers to the question of the liturgical experience. Theoreticians, practitioners and "consumers" must search for answers together. Only a team effort can bring the long twilight struggle of liturgical renewal to fuller fruition.

Included on that team should be those persons most experienced in *doing* the languages of worship: image, symbol, myth, and ritual action. Those persons are called artists. If we invite persons who are or can become artists of ritual to conceive, create, compose and choreograph liturgy in union with liturgical ministers and communities of faith, then the imaginations of believers are more likely to be opened to experience the mystery of Christ present in the assembly.

Aesthetic rituals, in contrast with those merely read as rote recipes, can create the conditions of possibility for evoking the experience of mystery—both in the liturgy and in the world. The artist knows how to activate the imagination through the sacramental principle, viz., the spiritual becomes present in and through the material—visible signs of the invisible God. Artists know how to take things from the material world—action, sounds/silence, words, movement—and extract them from their normal setting, turning matter into the bearer of spirit/Spirit. They can transform material realities into symbols by infusing them with feelingful insights into God's revelation which can be born in the artist's creative imagination as she/he encounters the world in the light of the Word. Surely only God creates the grace of communion with the divine and only God brings about transformation of consciousness and life in all people, including artists. Yet artists can create expressions which allow God's transforming grace to function more efficaciously.

All of this movement toward understanding the aesthetic nature of ritual finds support in the comments of a renowned thinker not normally associated with the religious dimension of life, the great American scholar and educator, John Dewey. In *Art as Experience,* Dewey wrote: "The ordinances of religion . . . are efficacious as they are clothed with a pomp, a dignity, and majesty that are the work of imagination" (Dewey, *op. cit.,* p. 326). The church, Dewey points out, has always, at its best, linked faith with the arts. Because of this aesthetic connection, he asserts, ". . . religious teachings were the more readily conveyed and their effect was the more lasting. By the art in them, they were changed from doctrines into living experiences" (Dewey, *op. cit.,* p. 329). Isn't that precisely the change still desired if "The Changes" are to bear rich spiritual fruits for believers—and for the cosmos?

Part II

THE IMAGINATION IN FAITH AND LITURGY

5

Faith and the Imagination

FAITH IS INITIATED IN THE IMAGINATION

Roman Catholic liturgy celebrates Roman Catholic faith. According to this religious tradition, liturgy is the summit and source of the whole Christian life. To understand Catholic ritual then, one must understand Catholic faith as lived. Faith is always offered to persons as a free gift from God. However, the offer of faith is incarnate. It is given through our encounters with other persons and events which serve as instruments for God's grace.

How then are persons prepared and disposed to be open to and receive the gift of faith? What part of the human person is engaged in responding in faith to God's self-communication? How does faith grow within the human spirit and develop over the ages within the community of faith, the church?

As was noted by John Dewey, faith is much more than a matter of fidelity to religious doctrines. Faith is first and foremost fidelity to life. It is life lived in the light of God's revelation in Christ. Such faith-life is daily influenced by the presence and inner pressure of the Holy Spirit stirring within believers.

Doctrines simply articulate conceptually what the life of faith means interiorly both to the community of faith and to individual believers. They are time-conditioned teachings which were created in response to particular questions raised at certain times in history. The development of doctrines continue through the living tradition of the church and individual believers. As is recorded in 1 John 3, 27, "As for you, the anointing you received from him remains in your hearts. This means you have no need for anyone to teach you. Rather, as his anointing teaches you about all things and is true— free from any lie—remain in him as that anointing taught you."

The life of faith peaks in that mountain moment called worship. As our tradition states, *lex orandi, lex credendi.* The church's belief flows from the church's prayer and worship. Faith and worship are partners. To understand how worship happens, it is essential to grasp how faith happens. Both are functions of the human imaginative system because both are concerned with a dimension of reality which cannot be seen with the eyes of sense or reason. Both deal with that Reality within reality which is God's presence; yet always a presence of One who is more than meets the eye. This reality/presence is the reign of God which is both *in* but not *of* this world.

Both worship and faith, then, are functions of the human imaginative system. The pivotal insight of these reflections is simply this: persons come to faith (evangelization) through the engagement of the imagination. Persons grow in faith (spirituality) through the functioning of the imagination. Persons seek to understand faith (catechesis and theology) through reason inspired by imagination. Persons celebrate faith (liturgy) through aesthetic forms of imagination. Naturally intellect, emotions and will are involved in the submission of faith. But imagination is always a crucial element in everyone's faith even if this is only implicitly acknowledged.

FAITH SHARED THROUGH IMAGINATION

In his 1976 novel, *Madonna Red,* James Carroll wrote of the relationship between faith and imagination. The scene centers around St. Matthew's Cathedral and the British Embassy in Washington, D.C. Father John Tierney, associate pastor, is preparing the daughter of the British ambassador to the United States to receive her first holy communion. The ambassador, not a Roman Catholic himself, says to Father Tierney: "Perhaps you'd understand what I mean, Father, if you had a daughter. Frankly I do not think Catholicism as it is now will engage her imagination sufficiently to survive into adulthood with her." The priest replies: "I think I do understand what you mean, frankly. . . . In a small way I do have a daughter. Yours. And the challenge of nurturing in her a religious, a Catholic imagination leaves me winded" (James Carroll, *Madonna Red,* NY: Little, Brown and Co., 1976, p. 81).

Today, anyone who attempts to pass on the Catholic faith, given both the state of the culture and the state of the church, must also feel somewhat winded. For what can it mean to nurture a Catholic imagination in a church struggling to survive in a culture so dominated by the secular. Yet it is indeed the imagination which is at the heart of the problem of evangelization, spirituality, catechesis, theology and liturgy in our time. We do not need new concepts or new arguments to convince people of the truth of God's revelation. We need not necessarily have more *words* as such at all.

As playwright Peter Shaffer puts on the lips of the tortured psychiatrist, Martin Dysart, in *Equus,* persons in this secularized culture desperately desire "a way to see in the dark" (Peter Shaffer, *Equus*). They want to be shown that belief in transcendence is both a reasonable, credible act and one that is humanly fulfilling. Belief becomes an incarnate possibility for such persons when they experience it in believers' expressions of love. Such love can engage the human imaginative system sufficiently to reveal the presence of the reign of God in this world, a presence which persons can come to trust unconditionally.

Proclaiming God's reign, permanent presence, in contemporary culture calls for a vibrant use of aesthetic forms, forms of imagination. Only such insights beyond the superficialities of our consumer-glutted society can reopen avenues into spiritual truth. Yet ours is, according to Archibald MacLeish, a culture experiencing a "crisis of starved imagination." Thomas Merton, too, sensed this when he wrote: "The lack of qualitative judgment, of taste, of personal discrimination, of openness to new possibilities, is bound up with one great defect—a failure of imagination" (*Contemplation in a World of Action,* NY: Image Books, 1973, p. 355).

On the other hand, the communications media has practically drowned our culture in rapid-fire images, inundating the imaginations of potential consumers with shallow, alluring images. Commercials, with their practical symbols of clean sinks and shining sting rays, of reveling in the Sta-Free bra and delighting in Fruit-of-the-Loom, open us to ever new possible materialistic modes-of-being-in-the-world made possible by the products of science and technology. Marketing techniques appeal to images of greed and control. The images get inside and transform us—not often for the good. The young son of some friends of mine always remembers the television commercials better than the content of Sesame Street. Why? Because, through such strong, persuasive forms of imagination, these commercials get inside youngsters who find their interiority conditioned by our image industries.

Christians as well must appeal to the imagination with the spiritually transforming truth of the good news of Jesus' death and resurrection. Strong, appropriate images of faith can bring a new energy to the gospel in our time. Paul VI, in his apostolic exhortation, *Evangelii Nuntiandi,* 1976 (henceforth referred to as EN) spoke of evangelization as "the essential mission of the church." He called for new methods and new approaches to make Jesus known as "good news." He rightly observed: "Man has passed beyond the civilization of the word . . . today he lives in the civilization of the image." (#42) People's imaginations need to be engaged to open up new ways of living together in the world. Consumerism does it. Why not Catholicism?

Christian faith is not simply an intellectual and objective assent to truths revealed by God. This propositional emphasis in faith, flowing from Vatican Council I (1869–70), has been surpassed by Vatican II. In this century, the church's preaching calls people to personally know and become committed to Jesus Christ as our Lord and savior. This is more than, prior to, and more important than knowing objective truths *about* Christ. *Knowing him* is more significant for faith than *knowing about him.* This happens first and best in the imagination as a form of cognition.

For several centuries Roman Catholics have tended to pass on the faith through rationally-oriented forms of catechesis and theology without understanding well and using effectively the prior and more imaginal processes appropriate for evangelization. Formerly religious education had tended to employ methods which pass on the faith by teaching truths *about* God and Christ, before the person had heard and personally responded in the heart and the imagination to the *person* of Christ who is proclaimed in evangelization.

Too often the church invites people to come to and celebrate faith by using models of communication more appropriate to catechesis and theology than to evangelization and liturgy. Such intellectually oriented models do not suffice for the character transformation which is what Christian belief and living is all about. In traditional catechesis and theology, words, concepts and syllogisms are employed to demonstrate and explain doctrines. In true evangelization, on the other hand, new possible ways of living are held out to persons through forms of imagination that stimulate their imaginations to see through the surfaces of this life to that new life believed to be *in* yet not fully *of* this world. For some years the Rite of Christian Initiation of Adults has been developing such "true evangelization."

JESUS AND THE IMAGINATION

Jesus was a master of the imagination in his ministry. The reign of God which he proclaimed is a reality truly *in* yet not *of* this world. It is already truly present, but neither directly visible nor yet fully present. God's reign has been fulfilled in Christ's death and resurrection, yet it has not been consummated. This kingdom, this inner working of God's Spirit in the world and within persons, cannot be perceived either by the senses or discursive reason. For this reason, Jesus appealed to people's imaginations to enable them to become aware of a reality which is more than meets the eye. By communicating through parables, images, symbols and ritual actions, Jesus opened people to see the visible world in the light of the invisible kingdom, God's hidden yet incarnate work to liberate and unify all creation.

Jesus did not use such imaginative forms merely as picture-making, make-believe or fantasy. Nor did he use them to enable people to escape from the reality of daily ordinariness. Rather, Jesus engaged imaginations so that people could get more deeply inside their own experience. He employed supreme fictions to ". . . redescribe our human reality in such disclosive terms that we return to the 'everyday' reoriented to life's real . . . possibilities" (David Tracy, *Blessed Rage for Order,* NY: Seabury Press, 1975, p. 207). David Tracy claims that such redescriptions of what is or might become involves ". . . a reorientation of our own most basic moods, feelings, reactions and actions, our very way of living in this world" (Tracy, p. 208).

Surely the preaching of Jesus is the best model for calling persons to faith. In his use of poetic metaphor, symbolic action, myth and image, Jesus opened people's imaginations to see and believe in the reign of God present in his person and mission. Those who followed him were shown a vision of life—a possible mode-of-being-in-the-world—disclosed to their imaginations through parabolic discourse. Such a non-conceptual, yet cognitive, approach to truth is in the very nature of all primary religious discourse.

In proclaiming the good news, why did Jesus, and why should we, use forms of imagination more than and prior to conceptual forms of discourse? Surely this is done neither to obfuscate the truth nor to confuse the hearers. Nor is this meant merely to ornament the truth in order to make it a more attractive package for contemporary consumption. Nor would one use aesthetic forms just to inform people of new facts which they could not otherwise know. Rather, such poetic metaphors are used in order to draw people *into the truth,* to *participate in the truth* which is being proclaimed. In this way the hearer gets inside the story told and the symbol presented. One can come to see the truth of reality from inside better than merely observing reality as an outsider. The gospel thus becomes not just facts to be known but opens hearers to a more direct experience of and participation in God's reign in the world as well. In this way the good news becomes internalized and evangelization occurs more efficaciously.

WHAT IS THE IMAGINATION?

Just what is meant by imagination? Very simply put, it is the mind imagining. It is what the mind does most of the time. It what the mind does most successfully. Imagination is not just another of the human faculties, like intellect, will and emotions. It is the *crossroads* of all of the faculties. Imagination functions to bring intellect, will, feelings and body together in a synthetic act of knowing: "Aha, that's truth!" Imagination, according to John Dewey, is the capacity to combine the old with the new so that it becomes "the chief instrument of the good" (Dewey, *Art as Experience,* p. 348). The imaginative activity which opens one to faith must be truly *an act of cognition,* a way of knowing.

Imagination gives birth to an insight into objective reality with subjective feelingfulness, not just logical or scientific accuracy. It is a way of knowing that fills gaps in our understanding for which words and concepts are inadequate. It is the way we come to know who we love and who we hate. It's that part of our knowing process which grasps our personal, psychic truth—the truth about our inner selves and all our relationships. It may be that still point-within which mystics refer to as "the heart," the center where Spirit merges and meshes with spirits as persons come to know God.

Discursive reason, through concepts and words, allows the mind to grasp and verbalize what was, what is and what *predictably* may be. But reason alone is incapable of transcending itself to lay hold of the *unpredictability* of mystery. The range of the mind-thinking is limited; that of the mind-imagining is less limited. Through imagination human minds can be radically opened to transcendence. Minds know more than can be expressed in concepts and words. We know more than we can say. Dewey wrote: " 'Reason' at its height cannot attain complete grasp and a self-contained assurance. It must fall back upon imagination—upon the embodiment of ideas in an emotionally charged sense" (Dewey, p. 33).

Imagination, on the other hand, is the mind functioning to open persons to new and unpredictable possibilities. Such real potentialities transcend what eye can see and reason alone can know, truths such as the kingdom which is in, but not of the world, such as life coming through death. Analytical rational knowledge, of its nature, separates reality into parts in order to comprehend it. Imagination's cognition is unitive and holistic. Samuel Taylor Coleridge suggests that knowing through the imagination involves a change of mental mode which allows us to see things as a whole rather than in constitutive parts. In encountering reality, the imagination, he says, ". . . dissolves, diffuses, in order to recreate" (Samuel Taylor Coleridge, *Biographia Litteraria*, chapter 13).

Lest traditional catechists and theologians cringe at what may appear to be a disparagement of reason and systematic thought, let me hasten to say that the imaginal mode of cognition is a complement, not a contradiction to the more conceptual way of knowing about the mystery of God. It cannot replace it. However, in religious knowing, the imagination ought to function both prior to, as well as subsequent to, the mind thinking.

As Paul Ricoeur points out: "The symbol gives rise to [critical] thought; yet thought is informed by and returns to symbol" (Paul Ricoeur, *The Symbolism of Evil*, Boston: Beacon, 1967, pp. 247–258). And the symbol to which knowing returns after conceptual understanding is a kind of "second naiveté," bearing a fuller sense of truth than when we first encounter it. Perhaps this can be equated with the kind of interior knowing expressed by T. S. Eliot in "Little Gidding" from *The Four Quartets:* "We shall not cease from exploration/ And the end of all our exploring/ Will be to arrive where we started/ And know the place for the first time."

As the poet Wallace Stevens held, we find ourselves more deeply transformed and more radically reoriented by "supreme fictions" than by the most careful analytic discussion of what is or what was or what ought to be. Like the villagers who listened to the Samaritan woman's tale of Jesus and then went to see him for themselves, those coming to faith today need to be able to say to those who have witnessed faith to them: "No longer does our faith depend upon your story. We have heard for ourselves, and we know that this really is the Savior of the world" (John 4, 42).

The power of supreme fictions allows for a multiplicity of referents. The great myths create space in which persons can walk around and find their own stories. "The story confronts but does not oppress; the story inspires but does not manipulate; the story *invites* to an encounter, a dialog, a mutual sharing" (Henri Nouwen, *The Living Reminder,* NY: Seabury Press, pp. 65–66). The new possible ways of living which faith discloses are most powerfully disclosed to the imagination through the lived witness of persons of faith in whom there is "an interior enthusiasm that nobody and nothing can quench." "Modern man listens more willingly to witnesses than to teachers, and if he does listen to teachers it is because they are witnesses" (EN, conclusion and #41).

A personal experience with such living witnesses led me to choose to become a Roman Catholic. One of my earliest and best friends was a member of a Catholic family with six children. The father was the town's dentist. Everyone loved to visit and play in their home. There was a spontaneity and a playfulness there along with respect and seriousness which made this place attractive to the many children who came there. Perhaps it was what we now call "the quality of life" pervading their home which drew us. As I became older, I realized that the joy and serenity which was theirs was related intimately to what they believed and where they worshiped. I wanted to share that too.

This family comes to mind when I read in *Evangelii Nuntiandi* about people whose lives are symbols of faith: "They radiate in an altogether simple and unaffected way their faith in values that go beyond current values, and their hope in something that is not seen and that one could not dare to imagine" (# 21). And now my faith no longer depends upon their story. My imagination has been opened to hear and see for myself that Jesus is savior and Lord. And that story is told and probed, celebrated and lived in the Roman Catholic tradition. Through that family's living symbol engaging my imagination, a new authentic possibility for being-in-the-world became a lure for me. Then and now, this faith is a way of transformative living.

FAITH, IMAGINATION AND J.H. NEWMAN

Many Roman Catholic writers affirm the importance of imagination in coming to, celebrating, understanding, and growing in faith. One of them, John Henry Newman, the renowned nineteenth-century writer and convert to Roman Catholicism, wrote profoundly about such imaginative apprehension of faith. Inspired by Coleridge, he contended that belief begins not in the notion or the concept but in the image and the symbol. We are moved to faith and to action, he wrote, not so much by notions but by what seizes our imaginations.

In the process of human cognition, Newman made a distinction between "notional assent" to truth and "real assent." The former is an armchair nod of agreement based upon the demonstration of the internal coherence and the intrinsic truth of a proposition. This has been the dominant, rational approach to faith for centuries in Roman Catholic catechesis and theology. Real assent, which Newman says is what happens in the act of faith, requires

that the assent be lived through action and the concomitant transformation of the acting person.

The assent of faith involves a coalescence of cumulative probabilities grounded in experience. For real assent to be rationally
credible, he claimed, it must first be credible to the imagination.
Faith cannot be verified unless the imagination first senses that
what cannot be rationally proved is nevertheless probable, indeed,
credible and true. This movement from probability to certitude
occurs when that which is probable becomes credible in the conclusion. It becomes real to the imagination although it cannot be first
known by reason. Such probabilities of faith yielding real assent
are not immediately demonstrated. They are, in actuality, grown
into over a period of time.

Certitude in matters of faith is a state of mind coming under
the imagination more than under discursive reason, according to
Newman. In judging the probabilities as a whole, one is led to a
certitude of undetermined intentionality. Prior doubts are dissi-
pated through successful appeals to the imagination. The certitude
of real assent can be lost, not by demonstrations to the contrary,
but through a comparable process of erosion. There can be no
instance in which the truth of faith could be simply shown to be
either true or false.

Newman was quite clear that God's claim upon us is made in
mythic or symbolic forms. He realized that, when we appeal to
what is imaginatively credible, strange forms of expression are
inevitable. And no less inevitable is the fact that our response must
be in similar forms of imagination, such as rituals. These forms, he
was aware, are highly ambiguous. Although they deal with what
may be conceptually inconceivable, the truth presented in such
forms is not necessarily self-contradictory or untrue. In fact, Newman holds that "their very ambiguity or paradoxical form is what
preserves them as permanent possibilities of experience, besides
somehow guaranteeing their integrity as ultimate explanations."

The doctrines which express and contain Christian faith are
developed in imaginative responsiveness to divine revelation. Newman, in writing about the development of doctrine, states that
believers, individually and collectively, turn the mysteries around
in their imaginations until suddenly they click into present aware-

ness. But that click will not hold indefinitely. It is variable and changing since "here below to live is to change, and to be perfect is to have changed often."

So important is imagination to growth in faith that Newman thought that anyone who could not understand the creative role of imagination in perceiving truth would regard a reform of belief as a destruction of his very sense of the world. Many Catholics had just such an experience in the wake of the developments in the life of the church after Vatican II. Minds were too fixed upon the way things had always been. Imaginations were not big enough to open to new forms of faith expression. This was most notably true with regard to the reform and renewal of the church's liturgy. (These reflections on Newman are based upon John Coulson, "Belief and Imagination," *Downside Review,* v. 90, p. 298, January, 1972, pp. 9, 11, 12, and 13. *See also* John Coulson, *Religion and Imagination,* Oxford: Clarendon Press, 1981.)

6

Liturgy and Imagination

Just as faith is *initiated* in persons through forms of expression which appeal to the human imagination, so faith is *celebrated* in ritual forms. Rituals engage the imagination in order to create the conditions of possibility for experiencing more than meets the eyes of sense and reason. Imagination opens persons to the presence of Presence, the mystery. As a structure of interrelated symbols in a constellation of patterned repetitive behavior, ritual communicates truth-as-presence. This happens through the embodiment and enactment of the given images, symbols, myths and ritual actions. In this way, rituals, enacted cumulatively for years, binds believers ever more profoundly to that communally funded meaning of life to which they assented in coming to faith.

Liturgy joins worshipers together in the sacred myth of Christ, not merely as isolated individuals and not only in the present moment. In worship we surrender our isolation, our subjectivity to the communal ritual rhythms which take us beyond ourselves and our times. In ritual we open ourselves to the assents of others' faith, past and present, for the sake of a future full of hope. Indeed, in ritual we celebrate the reasons for the hope that is in us by baptismal faith.

John Henry Newman wrote that, through sharing faith in common worship, we ". . . acquire a personal depth, which is both collective and historical; it embraces other people's assents as one's own, and it stretches back into time. This effects a personality change; and it is what is quantitatively new; we find ourselves by being in equilibrium with others now and in the past; the polygon of oneself expands into the circle of a world unseen" (John Coulson, "Belief and Imagination, *Downside Review,* v. 90, #298, January, 1972, p. 12).

This is possible because liturgical symbolic action yields, at one and the same time, a diversity of meanings for each individual within the assembly. The genius of liturgical symbols is that they are not literal signs but "polysemous" ones, i.e., ones with a multiplicity of referants (Cf. Bruno R. Brinkman, "On Sacramental Man," *The Heythrop Journal,* v. 13 (1972), pp. 371–401; v. 14 (1973), pp. 5–34, 162–189, 280–306, 396–416.

Preachers are aware of this from the responses of persons who compliment their homilies. When asking what moved the hearers, preachers frequently discover that what was heard was not what was directly expressed or intended. Yet what was heard was that person's personal appropriation and perception of the proclaimed truth. It had been symbolically disclosed through the preached word. The word functioned, not as concept or syllogism addressed to discursive reason, but rather as symbol engaging the imagination. The performative utterance of the homily had released the imaginative dynamism of the worshiper so that mystery was experienced as his/her own in Christ. The life of the hearer linked with the liturgy and life is seen in new light.

PRESENCE IN LITURGY

The liturgy celebrates, embodies and enacts a multiplicity of relationships and presences through which Christ is present: in the eucharistic species, in the ministers, in the sacraments, in the word and in the assembly which prays and sings. In addition to the individual worshiper's presence to self, the liturgy opens avenues of interrelationship between God and the individual and the individual and God, which takes place in and through the interactions of the many persons in the assembly present in Christ's name. (*Constitution on the Sacred Liturgy,* #7).

Matthias L. Neuman, O.S.B., explains how these interpenetrating presences are activated in the celebration of eucharist: "As my imagination creates a sense of self-presence, so will I seek to encounter a purposive presence; that purposive presence is given through the presence of the believing community and the presence of Christ in the host. These presences will reverberate back to increase and revalorize my original sense of presence"

(Matthias L. Neuman, O.S.B., *The Imagination in Theology,* Rome: Pontificium Athenaeum Anselmianum, 1976, p. 60).

This experience of interpenetrating presences also brings past, present, and future into a kind of simultaneity, a unitive balance. Søren Kierkegaard's words about imagination apply. Imagination, he wrote, is "what Providence uses in order to get men [sic] into reality, into existence, to get them far enough out, or in, or down into existence" (Søren Kierkegaard, *Journals,* p. 243). He also noted: "Without replacing reason, it [imagination] is the means of all the faculties being brought into 'equilibrium' or 'simultaneity' and the place on which they are united is existence" (Søren Kierkegaard, *Concluding Scientific Postscript*). The liturgical experience, at its best, can come to resemble this.

Both in the liturgy of the word and in the liturgy of the eucharist new modes-of-being-in-the-world, new possible presences, are disclosed as a project for the imagination to envision. The lived experience of Jesus and the proclaimed story of that experience become our own through what might be termed a "fusion of horizons." This merging of the Jesus story and our story brings about an aesthetic experience, according to Hans Georg Gadamer. Such, he contends, "is not just one kind of experience among others, but represents the essence of experience itself" (Hans Georg Gadamer, *Truth and Method,* New York: Seabury Press, 1975, p. 63). Jesus' horizon and meaning is understood by entering into it through the imagination functioning cognitively. The disclosure of spiritual truth in ritual is something that takes place by simply letting it happen through a surrender to the variety of aesthetic forms which engage the imagination during embodied and enacted liturgies.

An example may help to communicate my point. Among the various ecclesial celebrations of faith, the eucharist itself, as a ritual form of imagination, can open persons to the truth that is more than meets the eye, the truth of God's mystery transforming persons into communion with that mystery. Let me share my own imagination's experience of one particular eucharist celebrated in a small chapel in Tanzania, East Africa.

When I visited the Maryknoll Fathers' missions there in 1973, I concelebrated a eucharist in a small "kegango," or subparish, along with the parish priest and about thirty members of the Sukuma tribe. The church was a hut made of mud, straw, sticks and cow dung. The low grass roof touched my head as I stood at the old kitchen table which served as their altar of God. The people—many sick, all quite poor and uneducated—gathered around, both on the dirt floor and on the few kindergarten-like wooden benches.

The Swahili language was used for the celebration. Since I was the principal celebrant during the eucharistic prayer, I had practiced for some hours in order to make the unfamiliar yet proper sounds of Swahili. Fortunately this is a relatively easy language to pronounce, even though I did not know exactly what I was *saying*. I did learn what I was *meaning,* however, in a flash of insight as I took the symbols of bread and wine into my hands that day. The direct understanding of words and concepts, which accompanies the use of the vernacular, did not get in the way of meaning being disclosed.

During the words of institution, the eucharist symbol cracked open for me, as it were. Deep dimensions of revealed truth swirled through my mind and heart, or better said, my imagination. Lifting bread and wine for all to see and pronouncing the familiar consecratory words in an unfamiliar language, I did not just "understand" what I was doing. The fuller truth about bread and wine becoming body and blood was disclosed to me through the engagement of my imagination with that age-old symbolic action, eucharist.

As I looked across the eucharistic bread into the faces of my black brothers and sisters and raised the cup of blessing before them, a question stirred in my mind: Why me? Why am I so well-fed, well-clothed and well-educated, while these folks eat so poorly, dress so simply and are, many of them, unable either to read or write? By what strange accident of birth was I conceived and born on the rich fertile plains of Illinois while these people take their origin and eke out an existence in near-desert conditions, literally and figuratively? By what quirk of fate am I a citizen of the world's most powerful and prosperous nation and these are natives of weakness and poverty? Why me? Why me?

Through the power of my imagination, stimulated by bread and wine as symbolic forms of imagination, those ordinary things of the table dissolved and diffused for me, as Coleridge said, and a new vision of reality and truth was re-created. A change of mental mode allowed me to "see" these people and myself in a newly disclosed and holistic way. An equilibrium came about in my center-spirit (or is it Center/Spirit?). And I became more profoundly engaged with reality than either eyes or mind could penetrate.

I knew that day that I could not authentically take bread and wine into my hands and say, "This is my body, this is my blood," unless I was also saying to the people celebrating with me, "This is *my* body, this is *my* blood, and it, too, joined with Christ's sacrifice, is to be given up for you." We have been gifted to share, not to keep, and this we proclaim as the *mysterium fidei*.

Liturgy, therefore, engages the imagination through aesthetic forms so that worshipers may experience the presence of the mystery of Christ in the celebrating church. As John Dewey describes it, "the embodiment of ideas in an emotionally charged sense." (Dewey, p. 33.)

Part III

PRACTICAL REFLECTIONS ON
THE ART OF RITUAL

7

The Introductory Rites

Having discussed the aesthetic nature of liturgy as a celebration of Christian faith, we may begin now to explore an artistic approach to the chief liturgy of the Roman Catholic Church, the celebration of the eucharist. In order to create ritual as art, two things are required. First, it is necessary to understand something about *the nature of aesthetic forms in general.* How are they conceived, created, composed and choreographed? Second, it is necessary to be knowledgeable about *the purpose and nature of each of the parts of a particular ritual.* This includes the meaning of each of the parts, their internal coherence, and the flow of each of the parts into and out of one another. Such information can help ritual artists to create a liturgical experience of the presence of mystery which is both communal and personal, that celebrative experience which an assembly is meant to have as the ritual cumulatively unfolds.

Eucharistic liturgy is made up of two parts: the liturgy of the word and the liturgy of the eucharist, "two parts so closely connected that they form but one single act of worship. For in the mass the table of God's word and of Christ's body is laid for the people of God to receive from it instruction and food" (*General Instruction of the Roman Missal #8*, henceforth called G.I.).

The liturgy of the word begins with introductory rites which are preparatory for and secondary to the word. "The purpose of these rites is that the faithful coming together take on the form of a community and prepare themselves to listen to God's word and celebrate the eucharist properly" (G.I. #24). This rite is meant to enable participants to move from one place, feeling, mood, and experience to another. It moves us from our ordinary lives into another kind of time and space—liturgical time and space.

We bring into the sacred ritual the secularity of our lives in order to be enabled to experience the holy, present in all of life as well as in liturgy. These preparatory rites are a time for stepping aside from the ebb and flow of daily existence. Stepping aside is important, not in order to ignore the rest of our lives, but rather to see our experience from a higher vantage point. In this way we can become transformed over a lifetime. We learn and experience that "we have died and our lives are hidden with Christ in God." Not by accident is the liturgy called "the summit and source of the whole Christian life." It is meant to be a mountain-top moment, a time to see the valleys of our lives from on high, from the point of view of the reign of God.

The introductory rites are composed of five parts:

- *Entrance Music:* "The purpose of this song is to open the celebration, intensify the unity of the gathered people, lead their thoughts to the mystery of the season or feast, and accompany the procession of priest and ministers" (G.I. #25).
- *Greeting:* "Through this greeting the priest declares to the assembled community that the Lord is present. This greeting and the congregation's response express the mystery of the gathered church."
- *Penitential Rite:* The communal confession and absolution has several optional texts given in the sacramentary. It includes the *Kyrie eleison* which "is a song by which the faithful praise the Lord and implore his mercy . . ." (G.I. # 30).
- *Gloria:* "The Gloria is an ancient hymn in which the church, assembled in the Holy Spirit, praises and entreats the Father and the Lamb."
- *Opening Prayer:* In the name of the assembly, the priest sings or speaks this prayer which "expresses the theme of the celebration and the priest's words address a petition to God the Father through Christ in the Holy Spirit" (G.I. #32).

The purpose of the enactment of these five parts of the introductory rites is to create and evoke three experiences for, within and among the members of the assembly: 1) *gathering* people together in faith, 2) *quieting* them from the busyness of ordinary doings, and 3) *opening* them to the extraordinary presence of God within and among the members of the assembly.

How would ritual artists aesthetically conceive, create, compose and choreograph the introductory rites in such ways that these three experiences are made possible for the members of the assembly? Before making any choices of sound and silence, of movements and texts, ritual artists must grasp exactly what experiences they are preparing people for. The most important questions to ask are not "what opening song to select?," or "who will process?" or "shall the Gloria be sung or recited?" These are slot-filling questions. Answering them may create liturgy-on-a-page. This does not, however, address the aesthetical questions about how to energize a celebration in which the conditions are created for an assembly's gathering, quieting and opening.

THE ART OF ASSEMBLY

Ritual artists preparing the introductory rites must address certain questions prior to filling the slots on a liturgical planning page. For example: How can the ritual be so designed that the possibility is created for the assembly to experience the "many" becoming "one" for worship? How can the parts of this rite be interrelated to enable worshipers to experience an inner quieting and settling? How can the sense of rhythm between the parts be established so that the rite is not experienced as just one-thing-after-another? How will the flow of the ritual moments gradually open participants to the multiple relationships through which sacramental grace may flow: self to self, self to others, and self to God?

Each of the answers to such questions help to bring about both an energizing of hospitality in the assembly and a reverent space for engaging the interior prayer of each individual. If this is not the experience created, the introductory rites can become "sound and fury signifying nothing." The readings may begin but nobody has been prepared to listen. Let us examine then how ritual artists must deal with the preparatory rites.

First, the *Atmosphere of Assembling.* To aesthetically create the introductory rites, ritual artists must be concerned with blending and balancing the two experiential values which characterize the gathering: *reverence and hospitality*. In the past, Catholics have been accustomed to experiencing reverence in the liturgical space. Genuflecting, kneeling to pray, no unwarranted gawking around, and silence characterized pre-conciliar liturgical gatherings. But that traditional reverence now needs to be complemented by authentic hospitality, since it is the entire assembly, not merely isolated individuals, which celebrates Christ's sacramental presence.

An energy of hospitality needs to be set in motion before beginning the formal ritual. Hospitality begins, not only at the doors of the church, but also in the parking lots and on the church sidewalks. Formally, the establishment of reverent hospitality is the role of the ushers, greeters and ministers of hospitality. Informally, it must be also the task of each member of the assembly as he or she comes out of private relationships into the sphere of the larger family of faith in public worship.

The attitude of warmth and welcome expressed by eye contact, friendly words of greeting or just a smile can do wonders to create the proper attitude and atmosphere for gathering. This can turn a cold coming together of isolated individual believers into a celebrating assembly of faith. It may be advisable to consider having the presiding priest and other liturgical ministers present at the entrances to share with others in the art of assembly. After all, hosts normally greet guests when they arrive as well as when they depart.

Second, the *Aural Ambience*. Ritual artists must consider what ritual moments in this particular liturgy will involve music. Consider first of all what people will hear as they enter the worship space. Will music be played or sung as the people enter? What aural ambience is desirable for gathering, quieting and opening? Surely there is no single correct answer for every assembly and every occasion. Entering a space filled with music by organ, other instruments, choral singing or, in certain circumstances, taped music appropriate to the season or occasion can be fine tone-setters for the celebration. These can help to establish the feeling of that particular feast as well as setting a beautiful communal context for prayer and praise. To "hear" silence in penitential seasons can also be a good choice.

Whatever aural ambience the ritual artists select for the particular occasion, musical rehearsals, whether with the musicians alone or with the assembly, are the least desirable gathering experiences. Rehearsals can block both hospitality and reverence. Musicians should be properly prepared before the time of gathering. They should be present, prepared and in place well before the liturgy begins. Musicians arriving, organizing music and instruments in front of an assembling congregation, do not contribute to the reverence and hospitality of aesthetic ritual.

What would one think if, when arriving at a theater, the scenery is not yet in place, the orchestra is having one final "go" at its tunes and singers are vocalizing off-stage? To energize reverent hospitality in the worship space, rehearsals by music groups should take place *before* rather than *while* people are arriving. Practicing instrumental and choral music as people assemble gives the impression that the musicians are not prepared to receive the assembly. It would be a bit like cleaning the house while the guests are entering the foyer.

Third, the *Procession.* How should ritual artists choreograph the procession? Traditionally, the ministers enter from the back or side of the worship space while all others stand in place and sing. Everyone in the procession, including the presider, should carry song books and actually sing. Singing by those processing is observed most often in the breach. When the ministers simply "parade" without singing, the impression is created that the congregation's song is a welcome for the truly important people, the processing ones. It can resemble peons praising the powerful!

The function of the opening song is clearly a song to welcome the whole assembly, not just the priest and/or ministers alone. It is meant to create an experience of unity in a mood appropriate to the occasion. Song is the sign of the heart's joy. . . . Thus St. Augustine says rightly: "To sing belongs to lovers." There is also the ancient proverb: "One who sings prays twice" (G.I. # 19). Ritual artists should always choose music which will facilitate this experience of gathering, quieting and opening which is proper to the feast or season.

What music best accompanies the procession? Psalmody done antiphonally is the most traditional and perhaps the most appropriate music for the procession at mass in the Roman rite. Hymnody has been, for the most part, traditionally reserved to the liturgy of the hours in Roman Catholic worship. For a variety of reasons, however, entrance music has become hymnic more often than not since Vatican II. This practice needs reevaluation and revision.

Many people resist picking up their hymnals or participation aids to sing hymns during the procession and elsewhere within the rite. Why is this? Some may do so because they judge the music to be mere frosting on the liturgical cake. They wait it out. They don't want to be bothered until "the mass begins," which means, of course, when the priest opens his mouth. What they don't realize is that the singing is as much "the mass" as is the sign of the cross and the presider's greeting. Others may think that the hymns/songs are too long, too unfamiliar or too difficult. Still others may choose to be passive participants because they don't like to sing, think that they can't sing or just plain don't care for music.

If the problem is judged to lie with the assembly, catechizing the people on the meaning of full, conscious, and active participation in liturgy may help. If, however, the problem lies with the choice of the type of music for the procession, selecting the most appropriate music for that particular ritual moment and movement may be just as important as catechesis in order to convert standers into singers from the start. A steady diet of psalmody with congregational refrains as the entrance music can be both most traditional and most successful. When familiar psalm refrains are used during the procession, people seem to sing more readily and more willingly with gusto and spontaneity.

To use the same seasonal psalm refrain each Sunday during a liturgical season can be most effective. Not only does it engage more people in singing, it also can help to unify the liturgies of a season. The repetition of the refrain builds toward a season's climax. The refrain's cumulative power can be increased by adding new musical elements to it each Sunday. For example, begin Advent I by singing, "O Come, O Come Emmanuel" in unison. On each successive Sunday add first the organ, then harmony for the choir and finally descants by singers and instruments.

Different forms of the processional can be choreographed for special seasons and feasts. In Advent, for example, the advent candles for the wreath may be carried in procession and put in place during the introductory rites. If there is to be any notable acknowledgment of the wreath within the rite, blessing and placing the candles might be done in place of or combined with the penitential rite. Liturgical dancers/ministers of gesture might process, bearing and gesturing with one candle on Advent I, two dancers and candles on Advent II, three dancers and candles on Advent III, and four on Advent IV. Each Sunday, as Advent progresses toward Christmas and Epiphany, the light grows brighter within the assembly space. This can be a very effective seasonal addition to this part of the rite. The season is thus musically and choreographically connected around a traditional symbol. Liturgical linkage is always effective for gathering, quieting and opening the assembly.

In Lent, a silent entry and/or a shorter passage of entry can be effective to create the motif of the season. Another choreography would have the ministers sitting silently in their places five minutes before the liturgy begins. If there is a procession, the ritual artists may choose to have the Kyrie/Lord Have Mercy sung during the entire time of the processional. A particularly haunting effect can be created by using cantors stationed at various places around the worship space chanting this litany with the assembly. This can create a powerful experience of both imploring and praising the Lord's mercy.

If the priest sings well, he may wish to sing the first Kyrie eleison alone and unaccompanied from the back of the aisle. The congregation repeats this several times until the procession halts in the center of the worship space. Once again, as at the Easter vigil candle procession, the priest intones Christe eleison which is then taken up by the assembly. Finally, arriving in the sanctuary, the priest intones Kyrie eleison to which the assembly responds a final time.

After greeting the assembly from the foot of the altar rather than the normal place of presiding, all could be invited to kneel as the priest does so on the bottom step of the altar. All bow their heads calling to mind their need for forgiveness. After a significant period of silent reflection, they join in reciting the confession of sins which concludes with the priest's words asking that God have mercy, forgive sins and bring all to everlasting life. Only then would the priest stand, sing "Let us pray" and, after a moment of silence, sing the opening prayer.

For possibly still greater penitential effect, this too could be done facing the altar rather than the people. The people could either stand or remain kneeling for the opening prayer during Lent. At the conclusion of the prayer, the priest may wish to hear the word sitting in a front seat with the assembly. With such legitimate modifications of the introductory rites, a clear signal is given that a new season is being celebrated. A different modality is created for gathering, quieting and opening.

Quite another choreography is suggested for the Easter season. Since the Gloria is best sung, especially throughout these Sundays of Easter, the procession might enter with instrumental music or the singing of choral music. The Gloria would then become the "first" hymn, possibly sung during the sprinkling of the assembly with blessed water. To sing a large entrance song during Easter time, or any time for that matter, followed by a mighty Gloria can be experientially redundant. Two such "big" successive musical experiences may give entirely too much musical weight to the introductory rites which are, after all, only secondary rites.

A note to musicians: never introduce the processional music as a song "to greet our celebrant, Father Ponderous B. Portly." One macho-male cleric told me that the song leader in his parish once invited all present to stand and welcome the celebrant by singing "Hail, Holy Queen." Once as I began to process for a liturgy I heard the words of the song leader: "Let us stand and welcome our celebrant, Father Collins, by singing 'You Are Our God.' " As much as the lesser side of me might desire to be "God," and as much as some folks over the years have feared I was trying to be "God," I know that in truth I am not anyone's God! Whatever is spoken in liturgy must be clearly the truth!

Another note to musicians: when the opening song is announced, the organ or instruments should play an introduction which is of sufficient length to accomplish several things for the assembly: 1) to enable all to find the page in the book (a chord or short phrase are normally not sufficient); 2) to sense the rhythm of the song (the tempo should be set clearly with no ritard at the end of the introduction); 3) to feel the mood of the music (this is done especially by the registration of the organ and/or instrumentation selected as well as the tempo).

Fourth, *Selecting Emphasis or Weight.* The introductory entrance rites should not be created in such a way that each of the parts receives the same emphasis. "Great importance should be attached to the use of singing at mass; but it is not always necessary to sing all the texts that are of themselves meant to be sung" (G.I. # 19). "In choosing the parts actually to be sung, preference should be given to those that are more significant and especially to those to be sung by the priest or ministers with the congregation responding or by the priest and people together" (G.I. # 19).

A certain rhythm of highs and lows needs to be established within the introductory rites. The assembly should experience it as secondary yet as clearly preparatory and leading up toward the word. One part or another ordinarily should receive the greatest weight, attention or intensity while the others are given less emphasis. Movement and stillness, words, music and silence all allow those present to create that inner, quiet space where they can discover their personal mystery merging and meshing with the mystery of Christ present in the assembly, the ministers, the word and the sacrament. Too much activity, too much talking, and too much singing just do not succeed as a transition from many mysteries to the one mystery. Unless there is special emphasis given to one rather than equal weight to all of the parts, the rhythm of the rite is just plunk, plunk, plunk. It resembles just one darned thing after another—like reading a recipe.

An example: A ritual artist may opt to put the emphasis on the penitential rite during Lent. By singing the Kyrie as the processional music and by praying penitential rite 3 which confesses our sins to God, it is clear that we are gathering in the motif of the season and the introductory rites are thus weighted in that direction. It should be noted that the "Lord, Have Mercy" text is never used after penitential rite 3. Once is enough! One should be clear that "Lord, Have Mercy" is primarily a praise of God's mercy, not a focus on our sinful foolishness. Words such as "For all the times we beat our spouses, etc.," are not proper articulations of the meaning of this moment in the rite. Stick to words that call out who God is *for us* in mercy, not words which focus on our failures through sin.

Another example: During the Easter season emphasis should

not be placed on the penitential rite. Avoid this either by choosing its shortest form, or by reciting instead of singing it, or, even more appropriately, by eliminating it in favor of the rite of blessing and sprinkling of water. While any Easter or baptismal hymn, psalm or refrain may be sung during the sprinkling, it would also be appropriate to sing the Gloria. This would shorten the entrance rite rather than making it top-heavy in relation to the liturgy of the word.

Notice how this practice dovetails the ritual moments. Instead of having the blessing and sprinkling make an already over-weighted introductory rites even heavier, this thins it out and fosters good ritual rhythm. While respecting the basic structure of the rite, it places an emphasis on *one* of the rite's moments, rather than having equal emphasis on all of the parts. Settings of the Gloria involving congregational refrain and choir verses work particularly well for this purpose. Without needing to have their eyes glued to the music, people can watch the rite unfolding around them and respond with a sign of the cross and with visual contact with the presider while still singing the rite's accompanying song.

The procession of sprinkling can create a problem in ritual rhythm. It can appear to create two processions, one to enter and another to sprinkle. This is particularly true if the entrance procession has been accompanied by strong music. In such a case, the sprinkling gestures may seem like much-ado-about-nothing. Therefore, if there is to be sprinkling, the ministers might consider choosing, on occasion, a simpler and shorter form of entry which could be accompanied by instrumental music. Or they could be already in their places in the sanctuary area during the opening music. In either case, a procession of sprinkling with the priest and one acolyte or even with all the ministers would best be choreographed to move throughout the entire worship space—middle aisle and side aisles. To maximize this baptismal symbol calls for the sprinkling procession to move throughout the entire assembly, not just a "quicky" down the center aisle.

Fifth, the *Presiding Priest.* According to surveys of worshipers, the two key elements that facilitate good liturgy are first, the priest, and second, the music. The introductory rites facilitate many things within the assembly but much of the preparation for the word is the work of the presider. After the procession has symbolized "going up to the house of the Lord," and once there has been created the transition from ordinary time to liturgical time, and once the sacredness of the space has been established by song and gesture, and once there has been a shift from street conversation to ritual language, the burden of the rite rests largely upon the presiding priest as he greets the assembly.

More than any other factor, the kind of priestly presence established by the way he enters singing in the procession and his warm countenance can make or break this transitional time. The aesthetic effect of a rousing gathering song can be easily squelched by inappropriate first words from the mouth of the priest. His warmth in greeting the assembly with well-chosen words but not extensive verbiage invites people into the celebration. His body language, combining both smile and solemnity, sets the tone of reverence and hospitality.

Linkage words used by the presider are extremely effective in establishing continuity between the song and the greeting. First, a negative example: At the conclusion of the opening song, the presider should avoid saying, "Let us begin our celebration. . . ." Those words are false. The liturgy began with the opening song, not the greeting of the presider. Once again, the words spoken should be true to the unfolding of the ritual. Now for a positive example: If the opening song has been "Praise to the Lord," the presider's first words might be: "We do gather to praise the Lord— in the name of the Father. . . ."

The priest's body must speak as effectively as his mouth. His arms extended in welcome, his posture—erect but not stiff—his eye contact with the members of the congregation—all of these embody reverent hospitality and generate the same within the assembly. When inviting people into a period of prayer with "Let us pray," he should extend his arms as if to embrace all into the prayer. Then there should be a pause for silent prayer with the presider's eyes lowered in personal reflection. After some seconds, the priest prays with good verbal rhythm and with unaffected reverence in the name of all, avoiding the deadly sing-song tone.

The opening prayer, indeed all prayers, should be paced according to the rhythmed words as indicated by the separate lines of the prayer as printed in the sacramentary. In praying, the presider should not be glancing out at the assembly. The prayer is addressed to God, not to the people. At the conclusion, as he says "We ask this . . . ," it would be appropriate to gather in the assembly in his glance, thus inviting them to a full, resounding "Amen."

Presiders should keep in mind that the singing of the opening prayer can, at times, create a most effective climax to the introductory rites. A sung "Amen" is also a kind of exclamation mark indicating that the assembly has been gathered, quieted and opened for the proclamation of the word of God. On the other hand, nothing creates aesthetic dropsy after a rousing singing of the Gloria like a flat, recitation of "Let us pray" before the opening prayer.

Ritual artists who conceive, create, compose and choreograph the entrance rite in the light of these aesthetic considerations offer the assembly a sense of a rising arc. Beginning with the first words of welcome up to the first reading of scripture, the ritual should be experienced as a movement upward, toward and into the word of God. The rising rhythms of reverent hospitality set in motion by the ebb and flow of the parts of the introductory rites will either make people glad to be present or prompt them to peek at their watches wondering "How long, O Lord."

In such an aesthetically experienced preparatory rite, people can be enabled to experience their ordinary lives beginning to be lifted into the light of the word. Through being gathered, quieted and opened, the conditions can be created for believers to experience anew the extraordinary mystery present, not just within the ritual, but in all their waking moments. While this is only a secondary, introductory rite, its cumulative power can enable people to effectively enter into something of primary importance, namely, hearing and responding to the word of God.

8

The Liturgy of the Word of God

The principal elements of the liturgy of the word are the scriptural readings. All of the other parts are related and subordinate to the word of God. "The readings lay the table of God's word for the faithful and open up the riches of the Bible to them" (G.I. #34). "When the scriptures are read in the church, God himself is speaking to his people, and Christ, present in his own word, is proclaiming the gospel" (G.I. #9). "Christ is present to the faithful through his own word. Through the chants the people make God's word their own and through the profession of faith affirm their adherence to it. Finally, having been fed by this word, they make their petitions in the general intercessions for the needs of the church and for the salvation of the whole world" (G.I. #33).

The way the liturgy of the word is celebrated can either create an experience of God's presence in the word which can penetrate to the core of worshipers lives, or it can be experienced merely as a succession of words, words, words. As with the introductory rites, an aesthetic approach to the liturgy of the word must begin with an examination of each of the parts of the rite. Once the nature of a part and the interrelationship of the parts is explained, then ritual artists can conceive, create, compose and choreograph these several parts so that they are rhythmed to flow out of and into one another.

Music in Catholic Worship #45 summarizes the meaning and interrelationship of the parts. "Readings from scripture are the heart of the liturgy of the word. The homily, responsorial psalms, profession of faith, and general intercessions develop and complete it. In the readings, God speaks to his people and nourishes their spirit; Christ is present through his word. The homily explains the readings. The chants and the profession of faith comprise the people's acceptance of God's word. It is of primary importance that the people hear God's message of love, digest it with the aid of psalms, silence, and the homily, and respond, involving themselves in the great covenant of love and redemption. All else is secondary."

MINISTERS OF THE WORD AS ARTISTS OF PROCLAMATION

An aesthetically conceived and celebrated liturgy of the word calls for lectors, deacons and priests to proclaim and preach in the power of their own personal faith: not mere words but *the* word. This suggests, at its best, daily study and prayer with God's word prior to any liturgical proclamation. Faith-filled proclamation demands technical preparations as well. Six issues can be considered for ministers to prepare prayerfully and intelligently to proclaim God's word.

First, what did this particular word mean when uttered in its original setting and then later when it was recorded either by its original spokespersons, redactors or the community of faith? Second, how has the church over the centuries come to understand that word through its living tradition? Third, what does that word mean personally today in the life of the proclaimer? Fourth, what does this age-old message mean for those gathered in the living tradition of this particular liturgy? Fifth, how can the minister effectively, with proper techniques, execute this particular performative utterance of God's word, a word which is in the process of becoming one with the word of his/her own life in faith? Sixth, how can this personal appropriation of the church's faith by this individual minister be effectively uttered for the sake of the developing faith of this unique assembly?

Roman Catholics prior to Vatican II were not well acquainted with the Bible. Most middle-aged and older Catholics were bred on catechism questions and answers which quoted from scriptures to prove doctrinal points yet did not directly encourage persons to become familiar with the word of God in itself. The word proclaimed in liturgy was in Latin and so it was incomprehensible except through a translation in a missal and/or through the English repetition of the readings done by the priest at the beginning of the sermon. Sermons tended to be dogmatic, pietistic or moralistic lectures more than a homiletic breaking open of the word of God in relation to the lived experience of the assembly.

In the wake of Vatican II's stress upon the word of God, Roman Catholics are growing gradually toward a greater knowledge and appreciation of God's word in the scriptures. While doctrines will always remain of great significance for an authentic living of faith, Catholics today are also encouraged to study and pray with the Bible. Catholics need to understand that doctrines are rooted in scripture and the life of the church which is called tradition. God's word is not a set of statements. God revealed *God* as a self-disclosure in history, in the concrete lives of women and men, the people of Israel and the church of Christ. Before revelation was either in scripture or in tradition, it was first and foremost *an experience,* the experience of flesh-and-blood people. In the lives of real people from Abraham to the apostles, God was making divine, unconditional loving-kindness known through a promise that all people be saved through being made one and free in Christ.

Before being written down, revelation was first preached and lived by those who responded in faith to that word. This living faith, which includes doctrine, is what we call *tradition.* Lest tradition become lost over the centuries or become distorted through error, the experience of God's revelation to his people was repeated orally over the generations and eventually the word was recorded in print. These writings were collected over the years by the church under the inspiration of the Holy Spirit and are what we call *scripture.*

Both scripture and tradition contain and express God's self-disclosure and the divine will for salvation. Neither is complete without the other. What unites the written word of the Bible with tradition is the living, ongoing community of faith, the intergenerational gathering beginning from Abraham's act of faith: the church. It is in the liturgy that the church proclaims the word, not as a dead letter on a page but as a living tradition. In our prayer with the scriptures, both personal and communal, Christians come to identify with the saving events recorded there. To pray with scripture calls for an identification between the pray-er and the persons whose words and deeds are recorded in the scriptural narratives and parables. Those stories give us room to walk around and find our own stories. We become, through imaginative sympathy, the characters who heard Jesus. The same saving word speaks and wishes to act in our lives to bring about both comfort and challenge.

An example may help to make this point. A son-in-law attended mass one Sunday morning while filled with bad feelings toward his mother-in-law. The previous evening she had publicly humiliated him—one more time. Over the years of his marriage, this woman had treated him like an unwelcome guest in "her" family. In his anger, he had tossed and turned all Saturday night, nurturing images of revenge and feelings of hostility. This continued the next morning while he was at mass. He was physically present but his imagination was elsewhere—in images of revenge. Not until the reading of the gospel parable of that day were his hateful images and feelings challenged. It was the story of the prodigal son. This story helped him transform those negativities toward an inner conversion of vision, values and, eventually, behavior. He found *himself* in that parable. He was the prodigal son who needed to come home again. As he told me: "I knew I could not leave that mass without making a fresh commitment to try again to reconcile with that woman." The word of God had merged and meshed with the word of his own life, an experience which he had reluctantly brought to that Sunday liturgy. Surely no scripture scholar would have given that explicit meaning to the parable of the prodigal son. The preacher probably did not make that exact application either. Yet it was a link between God's word and the word which was made in the man's imagination inspired by the Spirit merging and meshing with his spirit.

Just as with this son-in-law, all must experience scripture as the living word. The word calls each of us to continuing conversion in the light of that word. Doctrines, addressed to the mind-thinking, help to keep conversion on the track with the truth. But scripture, engaging the mind-imagining, offers connected vitality and transforming power for our lives as we continue to put on that new being created in the image of Jesus the Christ.

To symbolize the presence of God's word, an attractive lectionary and book of the gospels should be used. Reading from a throwaway leaflet does little to convey a sense of the importance of "the word which lasts forever" (Isaiah 40:8). Since Christ is present in the word, the books of the word should be treated with the reverence similar to, although not exactly the same as, that accorded Christ in the eucharist. They should be carried with dignity in procession, placed upon the altar or ambo with reverent respect and not simply discarded on a shelf or chair after the proclamation. That is not the way ministers treat the eucharistic species after the distribution of the sacrament!

THE RESPONSORIAL PSALM

The responsorial psalm is on the one hand a response to the first proclamation of God's word. On the other hand, it is also the inspired word of the Lord in itself. It is a ritual moment for a meditative assimilation of the scriptural message just heard. In text and motif, the psalm prayerfully teases out the meanings and feelings of the reading proclaimed.

For this responsive, reflective experience to be created, the responsorial psalm must not be experienced as just another reading. If, for example, the lector concludes the first reading with "This is the word of the Lord" and then, almost without pause for breath, says, "The responsorial psalm. The Lord is my shepherd . . . ," the experience is one of recipe-being-read. It's like Eliza Doolittle's "Words, words, words . . . I'm so sick of words." An aesthetic rendering calls for a significant pause of several seconds between the readings. Then the psalm is begun, preferably by someone other than the lector.

Who leads the psalm? "The psalmist or cantor of the psalm sings the verses of the psalm at the lectern or other suitable place. The people remain seated and listen, but also as a rule take part by singing the response, except when the psalm is sung straight through without the response" (G.I. #36). "The cantor of the psalm is to sing the psalm or other biblical song that comes between the readings" (G.I. #67). As a last resort (G.I. #66 and #90), the lector may read the psalm.

It is seldom liturgically effective to simply read the respon-sorial psalm. The psalm is by its nature a poem, indeed a song. If it *has to be read,* it is best proclaimed in a poetic fashion rather than merely read with the same tone and pace as the previous scripture. The best way to accomplish this experiential shift is to use music during the psalm. This can be done in several ways. First, the psalm and refrain can be spoken slowly and prayerfully by a music minister while music is played softly underneath the poetic reading. Second, the refrain can be sung by all and the verses recited poetically by a lector, preferably not the one who pro-claimed the first reading. The use of seasonal refrains rather than specific refrains for each Sunday can facilitate even greater ease and spontaneity in the assembly's participation. Third, the refrain can be sung by all with verses sung by cantor and/or choir. Fourth, a chorale setting of the psalm may be sung by choir, cantor or by the assembly.

As the introductory music for the psalm begins, the music ministers should be conscious that the sounds they make are to arise out of the silence preceding. The music does not stand on its own. It is woven from and into the larger tapestry of the rite. Therefore, the notes should begin with a volume and intensity that is commensurate with the previous scripture and in tune with the spirit of the occasion. For example, a Lenten Sunday and Easter Sunday might call for a different kind of musical introduction to the psalm.

In order to avoid interrupting the reflective flow of the word, a simple, soft introduction normally can facilitate the ritual flow better than a loud chord played on instruments. For example, the refrain melody without the harmony might be played with clear pitches and a distinct rhythm, yet quite softly. Musicians should be sure to set the tempo with which it is to be sung. Avoid ritards at the end of the introduction which can confuse the assembly about when to begin and at what pace to sing. A musical coda, repeating part of the melodic material at the end of the singing of the psalm, can help to bring a more aesthetic conclusion to the psalm better than abruptly ending the music with the final note sung by the assembly. An instrumental chord which is held until it completely dies away can also add an aesthetic effect.

SILENCE

Silence is essential in creating the liturgy of the word as an aesthetic experience with an assembly. "Be still and know that I am God," sings the psalmist. Silence permits people to reflect on the word as it speaks to their lives. It allows the power of the word to transform those properly disposed, those whose imaginations and hearts have been opened by participating in aesthetic expressions. Ritual rhythm always requires stillness between sounds. There is a coming to rest between the gestures. Silence is like mortar between ritual bricks. It holds the words together and increases the possibility of experiencing God's presence through the word. Silence creates a hunger to hear. This presupposes sufficient instruction and experience of both the ministers and the assembly on the uses and value of silence. Without this background, everyone will suspect someone has lost the place in the structured texts!

Where are the silences called for within the liturgy of the word? First of all, silence is appropriate between each of the parts. There should be a brief silence between the introductory rites and the beginning of the liturgy of the word. At the conclusion of the opening prayer, people need to be settled and quiet before the first reading begins. Silence can create a sense of expectancy. This silent time can be created by having the lector sit in the front of the congregation and come forward after the opening prayer.

The lector should pick up the lectionary from the ambo (not a missalette or piece of paper), establish eye contact with the entire assembly, and wait for people's attention. Only then should the first words be spoken. The word is experienced as coming out of the silence which precedes it. And those first words by the lector should be exactly and only what the lectionary says: "A reading from the book of Isaiah." This is proclamatory language, appropriate to ritual art. Saying "Our first reading is a reading from . . ." is painfully redundant, explanatory language. Such phrases only add to the clutter of words and the anti-aesthetic experience. This creates the liturgy of the wordy!

Second, silence is called for at the conclusion of the first reading. Allow the lector to be seated for a few seconds before breaking the silence with musical introduction of the responsorial psalm.

Then break the silence with the music only gently, almost reluctantly, as mentioned above. Never jar the assembly out of the rite's
established experience of the assembly's gathering, opening and
quieting.

Third, after the sounds of the psalm have ceased and silence
again reigns, the second lector should quietly approach the ambo
out of that stillness. The *General Instruction of the Roman Missal*
suggests that, when two readings precede the gospel, there be *two
lectors* whenever possible. Again, out of the stillness which follows
the psalm, the next word from the Lord is proclaimed within the
assembly. After the second reading, a silence is created similar to
that which followed the first reading. The quiet is broken by the
musical introduction of the gospel acclamation.

It is wise to determine who will signal the end of the silences
and the beginning of the new sounds. The presider or the leader of
the music ministry may do so. It should be determined by a regular
pattern so ministers aren't gawking around appearing to wonder
who is to do what! Whoever does this should carefully observe
approximately the same amount of silence in each liturgy. The
congregation needs to become comfortable with the regularity of
these ritual rhythms. If the silences are too much, too little or too
erratic, the assembly will be jarred out of ritual consciousness,
away from open imaginations.

Fourth, a silent period following the homily can be appropriate. This gives people the opportunity to continue to weave the
word into the fabric of their lives. The length of this silence needs
to be aesthetically gauged by the presider, based upon his sense of
the assembly's spiritual "place" at that time. Some homilies, good
or not so good, are better moved away from relatively quickly.
Others call for more reflective silence.

THE GOSPEL AND ACCLAMATION

The liturgy of the word reaches a climax in the proclamation
of the gospel of our Lord Jesus Christ, the Word made flesh. The
word of God is always in the words of human beings. But, in Jesus'
case, he, in his very person, *is* the incarnate Word. The ritual
heightens and intensifies this proclamation by an acclamation of

paschal joy, the Alleluia! This acclamation is "both a reflection upon the word of God proclaimed in the liturgy and a preparation for the gospel" (MCW #55). Used in all liturgies outside of Lent, this is always a rhapsodic musical expression. Alleluia is less a *word* with a specific meaning as it is a Hebrew *sound* which expresses "Praise God." It is the perfect preparation for the gospel of the risen Lord.

The gospel acclamation should always be sung, never recited. If not sung, it is to be omitted. When only one reading precedes the gospel, either the responsorial psalm or the gospel acclamation may be used. Both are not required. The acclamation is music accompanying the procession to the ambo of the one who is to proclaim Christ's word. The procession is to take place *during,* not after the singing. To heighten this ritual moment, an ornamented gospel book is carried from the altar to the ambo by the one who is to proclaim. Acolytes with or without candles may process. Incense may be used on special occasions. All of this choreography heightens and intensifies this climax of the liturgy of the word.

As the acclamation ends, the proclaimer should be aware of the ritual energy and rhythm established by the music. He will do well to take a cue for his own intonation and energy from that energized musical acclamation. "The Lord be with you" should be spoken by the one proclaiming the gospel rather quickly after the last note of the acclamation and with the same energy and intensity. The eyes of the proclaimer should be on the assembly, calling their whole beings to attention in the presence of the word of the Lord Christ.

With this kind of rhythmed ritual of the word, worshipers are more likely to experience God's word, not just words. They will have the opportunity to experience the mystery of Christ connecting with their own personal mysteries. Their stories can become more consciously part of the God story.

PREACHING THE HOMILY

So important is the renewal of the office and charism of preaching that a recent document of the National Conference of Catholic Bishops points out that the primary duty of the priest is to preach the gospel. Ordinarily, Catholics think that the priest's primary purpose is to "say mass." Official documents since Vatican II indicate otherwise. Priests are primarily preachers. Even in presiders' embodied enactments in ritual, the priest is meant to make the good news of Jesus present in the church for the sake of the kingdom in the world.

This is a considerable shift in understanding from the pre-Vatican II days. In 1954 I was a Protestant college student interested in becoming a Roman Catholic. A priest pointed out to me then that Catholics have a great advantage over Protestants. The former have Christ in the sacraments. The latter have only a book and preaching. And one recalls that one could miss the "fore-mass," i.e., the liturgy of the word, and not be guilty of mortal sin. The word was quite secondary in Catholic worship prior to Vatican II.

How far Catholic self-understanding has advanced since then! Both word and sacrament are the presence of Christ, each in its own way. Both scripture and sacrament make present the saving power of God (*Constitution on the Sacred Liturgy*, #7). This reversal of the understanding popular before the council may appear at first glance to be a reversal of tradition. Actually the increased appreciation of preaching is drawn from the deeper well of Roman Catholic tradition.

Writing about the year 150, Justin the Martyr said that, after the readings, the bishops instructed and exhorted the people to imitate the things they heard. Like the eucharist itself, the bread of God's word was to be broken and applied to the concrete life situations of the people. The numerous homilies which have come down from that patristic period witness this strong homiletic tradition. During the Middle Ages, however, the nature of the homily as a living application of God's proclaimed word in liturgy was weakened. And after the Council of Trent, a strong emphasis on the importance of priesthood and sacrament led to a depreciation of the value of the word proclaimed and preached. Vatican II has restored the balance. The homily is once again to be an important and integral part of the liturgy of the word in every liturgical celebration but especially during the eucharist on Sundays and holy days.

The ministry of preaching the word will be explored more extensively in chapter 11.

THE PROFESSION OF FAITH AND THE GENERAL INTERCESSIONS

The liturgy of the word proceeds with the profession of faith, the Nicene Creed. In this communal action all respond to the word with a firm assent to the faith proclaimed in the scriptures and applied to life in the homily. All say: "We believe." Through ritual enactment and embodiment, the word of God has been made "flesh" once again in and for this living assembly of believers. The assembly's response to the word is not only an assent to doctrinal propositions but to the person of Christ present in that word and within the assembled believers. Choreographically, the priest should move from the ambo to the presider's chair before beginning the creed. He may choose to be seated for a period of silence after the homily allowing an aural breather after so many words.

The general intercessions conclude the liturgy of the word. "By this prayer, in which the people are to take part, intercession will be made for holy church, for the civil authorities, for those oppressed by various needs, for all mankind, and for the salvation of the entire world" (*Constitution on the Sacred Liturgy,* #53). The presider introduces and closes the prayer from the chair while someone else (lector, intercessor, music minister, member of the assembly, etc.) announces the intentions. It is best that the lector not do this since this confuses her/his role as proclaimer of the word. The intercessions should be read from the ambo or from the place of the music ministry if this is in front of the assembly.

The Vatican II restoration of this ancient prayer form was one of the most innovative reforms of the rite. To be successfully implemented, however, much greater aesthetic attention needs to be given to the way it is done if it is to be experienced as prayer. Too frequently it is excessively wordy, rushed and preachy. In such cases it is experienced as anything but prayer.

Attention to the rhythm of word and song can transform this ritual moment from unheard wordiness to true community prayer. What can be done to achieve this aesthetic, prayerful potential?

First, cut down on the words. The contracting of verbose intentions and expanding of the prayer response by the people can create the greater possibility for experiencing this as truly the *prayer of the faithful.* Intentions relevant to the needs of the day should be simply stated. God knows what we need. We say it so that we can acknowledge our needs. Be brief or no one listens. Too many words plug the ears.

Second, be careful about the content of the intentions. The intentions should not become mini-homilies, restating the points of the preacher's homily. Intentions which tout the latest social or churchy causes, particularly without reference to their gospel value, are equally ineffective. Everyone in the assembly should be able to honestly respond to these intentions as Christian values to be desired. This is not possible if they are too ideologically oriented. Intentions should express needs of both the universal and the local churches and communities. Prayers of gratitude are not appropriate as general intercessions. The eucharistic prayer is the thanksgiving.

Third, a combination of speaking, singing and silence can create the aesthetic rhythm for this prayer. After succinctly *speaking* the intentions, there should be a few seconds of *silent pause* for personal prayer. Then, out of that stillness, the cantor *sings* the invitation: "Let us pray to the Lord," or "We pray to the Lord." The assembly responds with a simple, sung response such as "Lord, hear our prayer," or "Lord, hear us." A choir could add harmonies to the response. After the sung response and before the speaking of the next brief intention, there should be once again a few seconds of silence.

The organ or guitar can very effectively create an atmosphere of prayer by playing very softly as the intentions are read and then accompanying the sung response. A choir humming can have a similar effect. Using a new sung or spoken response each week is *not* recommended. Such variety can become mere novelty, preventing the free rhythm and flow of a spontaneous prayer response. Worshipers put too much mental energy into trying to remember this week's unique text and the imagination is not free to float in prayer. Use of the same response with seasonal alterations can be an excellent way to make possible an experience of prayer during this ritual moment.

9

The Liturgy of the Eucharist

The liturgy of the eucharist is in four parts: the presentation and preparation of the gifts and the altar, the eucharistic prayer, the communion rite, and the dismissal rite. The general instruction describes the meaning of this second part of the eucharistic liturgy: "At the last supper Christ instituted the sacrifice and paschal meal that make the sacrifice of the cross to be continuously present in the church when the priest, representing Christ the Lord, carries out what the Lord did and handed over to his disciples to do in his memory" (G.I. #48).

THE PREPARATION OF THE GIFTS AND THE ALTAR

Like the entrance rite which prepares the liturgy of the word, so the preparation of the gifts readies the assembly for the eucharistic prayer. "The purpose of the rite is to prepare bread and wine for the sacrifice. The secondary character of the rite determines the manner of the celebration. It consists very simply of bringing the gifts to the altar, possibly accompanied by song, prayers to be said by the celebrant as he prepares the gifts, and the prayer over the gifts. Of these elements the bringing of the gifts, the placing of the gifts on the altar, and the prayer over the gifts are primary. All else is secondary" (*Music in Catholic Worship,* #46).

This preparatory, secondary rite of preparing the gifts and the altar is best experienced as a visual more than a verbal rite. Let people see what is happening and tone down the verbiage. For example, the priest is asked to say all of the words to himself when there is music. If any are said aloud, it is only the two blessings spoken as the bread and wine are placed reverently upon the altar and even these should be spoken quietly. After all the words of the liturgy of the word, the assembly needs quiet and a psychic rest in order to assimilate all that has gone before and to place their lives, transformed by the word, into the gifts of bread and wine. The crushed grains of wheat and grapes are the symbols of the joys and sorrows of our lives, brought forward to be joined to the sacrifice of Christ (G.I. #51).

The gathering and the procession of gifts should be carefully choreographed. It is strongly recommended that the ritual's texts and gestures cease during the taking of the collection. All sit quietly while the gifts of money are gathered from the assembly. This allows attention to be focused upon the act of giving without the distraction of congregational singing or spoken prayers by the priest. Instrumental or choral music may accompany this action.

During the gathering of the gifts of money, the altar is to be prepared with corporal, purificator, missal and chalice (G.I. #49). A pall is optional (G.I. #103). Note that all of these should not be on the altar prior to this time. Such vessels should be on a side table during the liturgy of the word. Ministers may effectively choreograph the spreading of the altar cloth, the placing and/or lighting of the altar candles, flowers and the arrangement of the gifts on the altar table.

When the money has been collected, the bread, wine, water, and money are brought forward by members of the assembly. "It is fitting for the faithful's participation to be expressed by their presenting both the bread and wine for the celebration of the eucharist and other gifts to meet the needs of the church and of the poor" (G.I. # 101).

The money and gifts other than the bread and wine ". . . are to be put in a suitable place but not on the altar" (G. I. #49). An effective way to choreograph the procession with the gifts involves having the gift-bearers come directly to the priest who stands at the altar facing the people. This enables everyone to see what is happening. After all, the true gifts are the people themselves represented by the gift-bearers. Presenting the gifts at the entrance to the altar area prevents many from experiencing the full significance of the symbolic action.

As the gift-bearers stand next to the priest at the altar, the priest takes the bread and prepares it by raising it a little and saying the berakah words quietly. Then he receives the wine from the gift-bearer and does the same after the wine and water have been mixed. Only then do the gift-bearers return to their places while the priest quietly and quickly continues with his private prayers of preparation. The briefer the better with this secondary, preparatory rite. What is seen is more important than what is heard.

A presentation song *may but need not* accompany the procession of gifts "which continues at least until the gifts have been placed on the altar" (G.I. #50). This need not be sung by the congregation, however. Choral or instrumental music may be preferable. Why? If the people are invited to sing during the procession and presentation of gifts, several less than fortunate things can happen. First, the words of the song can distract them from the "place" in their hearts and imagination where the liturgy of the word has moved them in faith. Each one needs inner quiet in order to properly prepare his/her unique gift as it has been brought forth from the depths of consciousness by the word. Worshipers need the opportunity for the word they have heard to make connections with their life experience. Then they can know more clearly what is their unique offering symbolized in the bread and the wine. Second, it is not easy to hold a book and reach for money at the same time. Third, since this is to be primarily a visual rather than a verbal rite, it is best to allow worshipers to watch the symbolic action of preparation, thus feeling their way into the procession of gifts.

After the gifts have been reverently received at the altar, "the gifts on the altar and the altar itself may be incensed. This is a symbol of the church's offering and prayer going up to God. Afterward the deacon or other minister may incense the priest and the people" (G.I. #51). The washing of hands is done by the priest "inaudibly" (G.I. #106), "as an expression of his desire to be cleansed within" (G.I. #52). Music used during this rite should normally be concluded during the washing of hands lest this secondary rite be unnecessarily prolonged.

THE EUCHARISTIC PRAYER

After a less heightened yet visually well-choreographed preparation of gifts and altar, the eucharistic prayer, "the center and summit of the entire celebration" (G.I. #54), can more likely be experienced as the center and high point of the entire celebration. A lowered rhythm during the presentation and preparation thus leads up to a higher ritual moment, "a prayer of thanksgiving and sanctification" (G.I. #54).

According to the General Instruction, the eucharistic prayer is the prayer of *the whole church,* giving thanks to God by joining ourselves to Christ in his paschal praise of the Father. "The meaning of the prayer is that the entire congregation joins itself to Christ in acknowledging the great things God has done and in offering the sacrifice" (G.I. #54). This is the faith and theology of the matter. But is this what is actually *experienced* when the priest prays the eucharistic prayer in the name of the assembly? This experiential question is the crunch question in every liturgical expression and experience. Does the experience reflect the theory? If not, what can be done to make the eucharistic prayer more an experience of *prayer* for the entire assembly?

The General Instruction describes this prayer as a time "for all to listen in silent reverence." On the other hand, all are "to take part through the acclamations for which the rite makes provision." The eucharistic prayers for children provide good models for more extensive assembly acclamations dispersed throughout the body of the text which are prayed by the priest in the name of all. Such interjection of acclamations in the four currently approved principal eucharistic prayers can be quite effective in achieving a sense of fuller involvement of the entire assembly. An extended sung Amen by assembly and choir can also give the people more of a sense of assenting participation in the whole prayer. Aesthetically, this should be experienced as the peak moment of the liturgy of the eucharist rather than centering that peak moment upon the priest's praying the words of institution and the elevation of the sacramental elements.

The heightening and intensifying of the eucharistic prayer can be more aesthetically accomplished if the preface and its dialogue are sung by priest and people. Merely reciting this beginning of the eucharistic prayer can create the experience of simply continuing the lower rhythms of the preparation of gifts rather than lifting the ritual into a higher rhythm.

Even if the preface itself is not sung, the Holy, Holy should always be sung by the assembly. The singing of the three eucharistic acclamations (the Holy, Holy, the memorial acclamation with its introductory invitation, and the doxology and Great Amen) is essential to lifting the eucharistic prayer into its properly heightened rhythmic expression and experience. Simple, familiar musical settings of these acclamations can be most effective at weekday liturgies. The recitation of the entire eucharistic prayer always flattens out that which is meant to be a "center and summit" experience. It turns the mountain top moment into a plain!

The presider's body language is an essential aesthetic component during the eucharistic prayer. The posture should be erect yet not stiff. The preface dialogue calls for arm gestures which greet the assembly and invite them into the great prayer of thanksgiving. On the other hand, the arms in the orans position during the eucharistic prayer should be uplifted, ample in gesture without being exaggerated in extension resembling a crucifixion. On the other hand, the old rubrical norm of never extending the arms beyond the width of the shoulders is a regrettable minimalization of the orans gesture.

The presider's eyes should not move around and engage the assembly during the eucharistic prayer except perhaps when the words of the prayer specifically mention those gathered in faith. The eyes are best kept upraised slightly above the heads of the assembly or, if necessary, kept upon the text in the sacramentary. Closed eyes are not recommended since this symbolizes that the priest is in private prayer.

The elevation of the sacred species at the words of institution should be minimal in gesture and length. Raising the sacrament only slightly above the altar table, possibly at eye level, does not overemphasize the institution narrative. Theologically speaking, the whole eucharistic prayer is consecratory and should be experienced as such by the assembly. Not exaggerating the elevation at the words of institution allows the elevation during the singing of the doxology and the Great Amen to be experienced more as the climax of the eucharistic prayer. At the conclusion of the prayer, the elements should be raised in ample but not exaggerated gesture and kept so until the end of the singing of the Great Amen. To place them on the table during the singing disconnects action from word.

10

The Communion Rite

The eucharistic prayer re-presents the sacrifice of the risen Christ so that his whole body, the church, may unite their dying and rising with the Lord's death and resurrection. The Great Amen, the resounding assent of all to the words prayed in their name by the priest, leads the ritual from its peak rhythm into the less heightened tones and rhythms of the communion rite, "the paschal meal" (G.I. #56), in which the sacrifice of Christ, the whole Christ, is shared in a sacred banquet.

This rite has eight parts: The Lord's Prayer with embolism and doxology; the rite of peace; the breaking of bread during the singing of the litany, the Lamb of God; the private prayers of preparation by priest and people; the showing of the eucharistic species; the distribution of the body and blood of Christ; the communion meditation; and the prayer after communion.

While this rite is surely intended to be a communal expression and experience, a more meditative, personal but never private atmosphere needs to be created aesthetically. All of the parts of this rite compenetrate to create the conditions for believers to enter into communion with the risen Christ *and* with one another. Two equally valid and significant emphases need to be respected by the ritual artists who prepare the communion rite: they are the communal and the personal.

The first emphasis in the creation of the rite must be communal. The reception of holy communion is not merely a private "me-and-Jesus" event of intimacy. It is an experience of the unity of the faith community in the risen savior who is present through the Holy Spirit in all of the baptized and throughout all creation. In the sacrament of the Lord's body and blood, we become one with him and with each other, both in the present assembly and in the church universal. Sharing the same food and drink with believers around the world joins us with Christ's church everywhere.

The second emphasis is personal. This does not mean private. The communion rite needs to be so conceived, created, composed and choreographed that more than just the communal experience is embodied and enacted. It must also be so rhythmed that each individual's needs for quiet, intimate speaking with the Lord are respected. As John Paul II wrote in *Domenicae Coenae,* the reception of communion is "a manifestation of worship of Christ, who in eucharistic communion, entrusts himself to each one of us, to our hearts, our consciences, . . . and our mouths, in the form of food."

Prior to Vatican II, this private emphasis practically excluded the communal experience of communion. Since the council, however, the opposite extreme has too often been the experience. The communal emphasis sometimes regrettably eliminates not only the private but the personal experience as well. As is frequently the case in Christian belief and practice, either/or must become both/and. Both communal and personal moments can be present within the communion rite while realizing that the *purely* private experience does not belong within the liturgical experience.

THE LORD'S PRAYER

Let us examine the parts of this rite and their interrelationship to discover how this balance between communal and personal may be created.

The Lord's Prayer is the communal, prayerful preparation for sharing in the eucharistic sacrificial banquet. It is "a petition both for daily food, which for Christians means also the eucharistic bread, and for the forgiveness of sin, so that what is holy may be given to those who are holy" (G.I. #56a). While the prayer *may* be sung by all, and should never be sung only by an individual or by a choir alone, it may be best to recite the Lord's Prayer rather than sing it on most occasions. The reason for this suggestion relates to the ritual rhythm. After the full singing of the eucharistic acclamations, the recitation of the Lord's Prayer can be a nice change of tone and pace, reflecting, indeed creating, a movement into a new ritual moment. It also makes it possible for those who do not sing and those unfamiliar with the music to participate.

The assembly's experience of the eucharistic prayer ideally has been more heightened, more intense, more verbal for the priest and more silent for the assembly. Now the assembly prays together but in a less heightened and more contemplative mode as it prepares for the culmination of the sacrifice in the sacred meal. It is surely a communal rite but it must also remain truly personal. Lowering the level of intensity by reciting the Lord's Prayer rather than singing it can be an aesthetically appropriate beginning as the communion rite begins.

When the Lord's Prayer is sung, a unification of this ritual moment into a single piece is aesthetically created if, after the prayer is sung by all, the embolism developing the last petition of the Lord's Prayer (cf. G.I. #56a) is also sung by the priest with the doxology sung by all. To sing only the prayer and recite the embolism and doxology is a disjunctive experience. They are meant to be experienced together. They are a single ritual moment.

THE RITE OF PEACE

The rite of peace is described as follows: "Before they share in the same bread, the faithful implore peace and unity for the church and for the whole human family and offer some sign of their love for one another" (G.I. #56). The specific modes of exchanging the sign of peace are left to local usage (Appendix to G.I. #56b). However it is done, it should be experienced as a symbolic gesture pointing to a true interior unity among believers. The sacramental, ritual gesture makes present in the ritual experience the unity and love of the Lord uniting all by grace. At the same time the peace greeting invites to a deeper unity in the Lord through eating and drinking together at the sacrificial meal.

As such, the peace greeting both proclaims a unity that already exists in faith as well as being a symbol of a greater unity to come. By pressing flesh, the assembly enfleshes a spiritual unity in and through the offer and acceptance of forgiveness. Such peace is always more than just a human wish. It is a share in Christ's peace, a peace that surpasses all understanding, a peace which can be given by God but never achieved by us. It is the peace of the risen Lord present in and through the ritual embodiment of the Lord's people.

The Hebrew word, *shalom,* means a fullness of life and prosperity flowing from our being at one with nature, with self and others and with God. "Since the risen Christ is the source of all peace, this gesture expresses faith that Christ is present in the assembly. It is both a call to reconciliation and unity as well as a seal which ratifies the very meaning of a eucharistic assembly whose membership find and pray for peace in one another" (*Mystery of Faith,* p. 99). This prayer and greeting of peace are ritual expressions and experiences which are different than the "hi, how 'ya doing" greetings exchanged by acquaintances on the street. This is not a hoopla time nor a hail-fellow/lady well-met moment. It is meant to be a ritual human expression and experience, at the same time formal yet warm.

The priest is to greet only those near him in the altar area. He should not proceed through all or parts of the assembly area. "The priest may give the sign of peace to the ministers" (G.I. #112). If the priest moves through the aisles greeting everyone, the impression could be given that this greeting is something coming from the ordained rather than freely shared with one another by the baptized. The presider's greeting of many people also unnecessarily prolongs this rite. While he speaks and greets, others stand, wait and wonder why! However, weddings and funerals may be exceptions to this Rome-given rule of ritual restraint during the rite of peace. On such family-oriented occasions, the priest appropriately may choose to greet the families in the front rows.

Those in the assembly also should limit their greetings of one another, in most instances, to those nearest them. Any extensive verbal and bodily interaction by priest and/or people at this time disrupts the ritual's rhythm of communal contemplation. This reflective experience should not be interrupted by street-talk and country-club gestures. The greeting of peace is, once again, a ritual gesture. As such it deserves to be exchanged with a blend of both personal warmth and ritual restraint. Simple words, not extended conversations, are called for. "Peace be with you. And also with you," says it best within the context of ritual.

A story about the greeting of peace. A colleague of mine was
a newcomer at a particular parish Sunday liturgy. She arrived
alone, entering the pew in silence. The liturgy, she said, was an
appropriate blend of the communal and the personal. But, at the
rite of peace, there was almost no interaction between the members of the assembly. So the priest took the opportunity to inter-
rupt the ritual flow with an explanation of the rite. He urged the
people to make an extra effort to say hello to one another and to
introduce themselves. My friend turned to the man on her right,
extended her hand with a smile. He returned her smile and said:
"Isn't this a lot of baloney?" After generations of private praying
during mass, it will remain a long, ongoing task to change individual Roman Catholic pray-ers into communities of worshipers.
Should such an inhospitable person be judged to be a wrathful
reactionary? Not necessarily. There is a lesson in this reaction.

Ritual artists and scholars need to take seriously what members of the assembly experience, even if it doesn't reflect "good"
liturgical theory and law. What our revised rites look like and feel
like to members of the assembly is evidence as valuable as the
historical evidences for the proper placement of the rite of peace
from the early fifth century in the churches of Rome and Carthage.
Therefore, if someone experiences "a lot of baloney" during the
peace greeting, this may indicate problems with the rite itself: its
placement within the entire eucharistic ritual or the way in which
the rite is embodied and enacted. In this way both the evidence of
authority (historical, theological, and legal) and authority of evidence (the baloney) are respected.

The time is past when we can claim a liturgical practice "right
and proper" simply because experts tell us "this is the way it always
was," or "this is the only way it ought to be today." At least such
should not be the case when it comes to the historically flexible
practices of our liturgy. One can't justify a rite merely because it
copies an original ritual, either in its text or in its placement within
the ritual. One cannot justify a rite by giving only its theological
justification. "To express their love for one another and beg for
peace and unity in the church and with all mankind" are surely
sound theological reasons behind the peace ritual. But this leaves
unanswered the most important question: What is the *experience*

of the rite within today's liturgical assemblies? How does it flow from what preceded and flow into what follows? Does it add to a compenetration and a rhythmed flow throughout the entire communion rite or is it a standout piece of its own, disrupting the integrated ritual rhythm?

The only place to learn the answers to such questions is from the data garnered primarily from the experience of worshipers. The baloney-sayers as well as the yes-sayers must be heard. These know from the *inside* of the experience, not just from the *outside* evidence of history, theology and law. Although reactions to the rite of peace have been mixed, most people have become accustomed to and genuinely appreciate this tactile reaching out to one another in peace before being joined together sacramentally in communion. Most seem pleased that something "personal" does go on in our formal rituals.

The baloney response may express more of a dissatisfaction with the placement of the peace greeting than a rejection of the practice itself. An overly-extended and excessively exuberant peace greeting interrupts the communion rite's intended focus on personal interiority within the communal experience. Peace greetings then become a sudden call for external interaction, reversing the interiority which the aesthetic rhythms of the liturgy have thus far made possible. Once again it should be stressed that the communion rite is intended to be neither a private nor an isolated experience. Nevertheless, it does call for individuals to contemplate the mystery which is made sacramentally present within the action of the entire assembly. As always, ritual "truth" comes in balancing and blending, holding in creative tension what may appear to be opposites.

The possible problem of placement raises certain aesthetic questions. Does the greeting of peace always have to take place during the rite of peace? No, it is optional (cf. G.I. #56b and 112). The rite may mean more if done less frequently. It may also be located elsewhere within the rite. Where it is placed gives it meaning and helps create the kind of experience it will be.

For example, if the greeting of peace is done during the introductory rites, it can become an experience of hospitality which will build community for the sake of that particular liturgy. The community will sense the symbolization, the making present in sign, of warmth and welcome.

In another context, people might be invited to exchange the peace greeting at the conclusion of a homily about reconciliation as a sacramental enactment of the meaning of forgiveness. As still another example of a change of placement, the greeting of peace could be placed prior to the preparation of gifts which would symbolize the gospel exhortation: "Before you bring your gifts to the altar, go and make peace with your brothers and sisters."

Once again, wherever and whenever this sign of peace is exchanged, it should be experienced as a gift shared by the baptized, not one extended from the presiding priest. In 1977, the U. S. Bishops' Committee on the Liturgy made a clear statement about this. "Neither the people nor the ministers need try to exhaust the sign by attempting to give the greeting personally to everyone in the congregation or even to a great number of those present. . . . Unless the sign of peace is clearly tailored to a specific occasion, such as a marriage, ordination, or some small intimate group, the more elaborate and individual exchange of peace by the celebrant has a tendency to appear clumsy. It can also accentuate too much the role of the celebrant or ministers, which runs counter to the true understanding of the presence of Christ in the entire assembly" (*Mystery of Faith*, p. 98).

THE BREAKING OF BREAD WITH THE LAMB OF GOD

Some ritual songs exist for their own sake within the ritual context. They are independent of any particular gestures or movements. They stand on their own to be sung. Such include the Lord Have Mercy, the Gloria, the responsorial psalm, the eucharistic acclamations, and the Lord's Prayer. Other songs exist to accompany ritual actions and are not independent musical moments. These include all of the processional chants and the Lamb of God. The latter is "a litany-song to accompany the breaking of the bread, in preparation for communion. The invocation and response may be repeated as the action demands" (*Music in Catholic Worship*, #68). Since it is a litany, a song, its nature is best respected when it is done with a musical setting. Recited litanies can be dull, rote, and increasingly meaningless experiences for a liturgical assembly.

As the priest ends his participation in the rite of peace, he begins to slowly and reverently break the eucharistic bread and pour the sacramental wine which have become the sacrificed Lamb of God. The assembly should be able to *see* the elements being divided for the distribution of the sacrament. The breaking of the bread gesture of Christ at the last supper gave the entire eucharistic action its name in apostolic times. "This rite is not simply functional, but is a sign that in sharing in the one bread of life which is Christ we who are many are made one body [see 1 Cor 10: 17]" (G.I. #56c).

The singing of the Lamb of God litany should begin immediately as an accompaniment to the act of breaking the bread. This effectively brings an end to the assembly's greeting of peace lest it become too prolonged and interruptive of the ritual flow. The singing draws the assembly back into the rhythm of communal contemplation of the mystery being celebrated and received in communion. The Lamb of God may be a choral composition or one involving the assembly at least in the "have mercy on us" response. "This invocation may be repeated as often as necessary to accompany the breaking of the bread" (G.I. #56e). However, the singing should not extend much beyond the action of preparing the sacramental elements lest the ritual flow be delayed.

The fraction rite should be effectively visualized and choreographed for the assembly. All should experience the enactment of what Jesus did at the last supper: take, bless, break and share. The bread *taken* in the preparation of gifts and *blessed* in the eucharistic prayer is *broken* in the fraction rite to be *shared* as bread-become-body/wine-become-blood in the communion rite.

This preparation of the sacrificial meal can be enhanced aesthetically if the priest's breaking/pouring gestures are physically large enough and temporally long enough for the people to notice the significance of the action. The visual symbol is most effective when the bread resembles real food. It should be large enough to be broken into many pieces and the assembly should be able to see the wine being poured. Following the prayers of preparation by priests and people, the body of Christ is shown to the assembly.

For a fuller sacramental sign, the vessel of wine may also be lifted up with the host being held above the vessel.

THE DISTRIBUTION OF COMMUNION

The distribution of communion involves careful choreography and properly selected musical compositions. First, the choreography. Organizing the various eucharistic ministers is crucial to the rhythmic flow of the ritual. If ritual rhythm can be easily violated, it can for sure occur at this moment. Too much time is consumed during the communing of the many ministers. This confusion of movement can be due either to a lack of consistent and careful choreography, or to a lack of understanding of that choreography on the part of the ministers. A consistent pattern should be developed which is followed by all of the ministers for each celebration.

One approach which works effectively will be described. The extraordinary ministers of eucharist are seated in the assembly. They are thus visible to all as part of the assembly rather than ministers apart from or over against the gathered believers. This is made more evident when they come from the congregation to minister at the appropriate moment. At the beginning of the peace greeting, they move from their seats in the assembly toward the altar. Standing around the altar and facing the assembly, each minister is greeted by the priest. Then they greet one another as well as other ministers in that area. They then form a line or semicircle behind the priest and facing the assembly, or on either side of the altar facing toward the priest. They may also stand on both sides of the altar.

The priest may choose to place the host in the ministers' hands during the singing of the Lamb of God. This facilitates the movement and eliminates unnecessary time during the distribution. As the Lamb of God ends, the priest shows the eucharistic elements to the assembly after which all ministers communicate at the same time. The priest then receives the blood of Christ and next gives the vessels to two or more ministers who receive and then communicate the other ministers. Immediately all move together to the communion stations.

Both of the eucharistic species should be made available to

the assembly at all celebrations. There is no longer any limitation on the reception of the eucharist under both kinds, bread and wine, body and blood. The G.I. #56h states: "It is most desirable that the faithful receive the Lord's body from hosts consecrated at the same mass and that, in the instances when it is permitted, they share in the chalice. Then, even through the signs, communion will stand out more clearly as a sharing in the sacrifice actually being offered."

Second, musical composition. The G.I. and MCW speak of the communion song being sung during the distribution in order to foster a sense of unity within the assembly. "Its function is to express outwardly the communicants' union in spirit by means of the unity of their voices, to give evidence of joy of heart, and to make the procession to receive Christ's body more fully an act of community" (G.I. #56i). It begins when the priest takes communion and continues for as long as seems appropriate while the assembly receives the body of Christ. The communion song is sung by the choir alone or by the choir or cantor with the congregation.

The music selected may be from any good musical resource. "The communion song should foster a sense of unity. It should be simple and not demand great effort. It gives expression to the joy of unity in the body of Christ and the fulfillment of the mystery being celebrated" (Appendix to G.I. #56i). The most appropriate texts, according to G.I. and MCW #62, are seasonal in nature. Marian music or nationalistic songs are not appropriate. Topical songs may be used during ordinary time provided they do not conflict with the paschal character of every Sunday. The specified antiphon is recited *only* if no communion song is sung. If eucharistic texts are used for singing, they should *not* emphasize eucharistic adoration. This is more appropriate as Benediction music. Rather, eucharistic texts should speak of the sacrificial and sacramental sharing that is taking place in the sacred meal.

Music can enhance both the personal and the communal experience of the distribution of the sacrament. Instrumental and/or choral music are perhaps most suited to creating the best atmosphere for prayerful, personal reception. If worshipers are to be invited to sing, psalms or songs with familiar assembly refrains and cantor/choral verses are more effective. Rarely is the singing of songs by the full assembly effective during this ritual moment. People usually prefer personal reflection and resist carrying books or participation aids. Many communicants indicate by their silence that they prefer to be quiet as they receive the eucharistic Lord.

This lack of sung participation annoys many liturgical experts and some pastoral ministers. They point to the fact that a communion song is called for. Therefore people should sing. Historically, singing by the people took place during the distribution as long ago as the fourth century. Therefore, as an ancient tradition, it should be done in the reformed rites today. All that actually proves is: "That's the way it *was* done." It proves nothing about what is most effective and prayerful *now*.

The living tradition of today's worshipers' experiences must be respected as well as the historical precedent. We must learn from the experience of the past quarter century as well as from the fourth century if liturgical renewal is to continue to flourish in our time. History, theology and law were invaluable in getting worship reform off to a good start after Vatican II. But now the evidence of our own liturgical experience must be given ever greater weight as the renewal continues. If people who normally sing rather fully during other parts of the liturgy choose to be quiet during the distribution of the eucharist, perhaps their praxis is correcting theory.

After or near the end of the distribution of communion, the music ceases. A period of silence most effectively follows as the priest returns to the chair (G.I. #56j and 121). After so much sound in the assembly during the distribution, silence is a most appropriate experience for the next few moments. The priest, in determining the length of the silent period, should be aware that most of the worshipers have already experienced a significant silence during the distribution. The quiet period after distribution should be neither painfully prolonged nor ridiculously brief.

G.I. #56j states: "After communion, the priest and people may spend some time in silent prayer. If desired, a hymn, psalm, or other song of praise may be sung by the entire congregation." If instrumental and/or choral music rather than assembly singing have accompanied the communion procession, and worshipers have experienced sufficient personal reflection during the time of distribution, a communal musical expression may be most appropriate at this time. A choral meditation might be appropriate if the people have sung during the distribution.

During festive liturgies and even during ordinary time, this music after communion can be a kind of high hymn of praise. In such cases, the priest may wish to invite all to stand to sing. During Advent, Lent and other more subdued celebrations, a communion meditation-type music can be very effective when sung, possibly with all seated or kneeling. If, on the other hand, the assembly has sung a communion song already, it probably would be advisable to permit personal reflection during a period of silence after the distribution rather than to "over-musicalize" the communion rite with another song.

At the end of the silence or hymn of praise or communion meditation, the priest says, "Let us pray" and the communion rite closes with the prayer after communion in which "the priest petitions for the effects of the mystery just celebrated, and by their acclamation Amen the people make the prayer their own (G.I. #56k). Common sense, together with a sense of ritual rhythm and choreography, suggest that the tone and energy used in this invitation be sung or spoken in harmony with the tone of the preceding experience.

If, for example, the distribution of communion was followed by a period of silence, then "Let us pray" might be done very quietly while the priest is still seated. Then he would stand and, without any further silent reflection, speak the words of the prayer after communion in a meditative fashion which grows aesthetically out of the previous silence. If, on the other hand, all have been standing for a hymn of praise, the tone used for "Let us pray" should reflect the tenor of that hymn.

The priest may wish to use very brief linkage words in his invitation into the prayer after communion. These are a word or two or perhaps an image just expressed in the text of the previous music which would lead into the prayer after communion. Such linkage words help to tie ritual rhythm together and aid in the experiential flow of the ritual. They help worshipers to experience the cumulative unfolding of the ritual moments rather than sensing that the ritual is just one thing after another without rhyme, reason or rhythmed connections. The presider might also link the silence by saying "Let us continue in prayer," since presumably all are already praying.

Should the prayer after communion be sung? It may be either sung or recited. If the priest has sung the opening prayer, singing this prayer could provide a sense of continuity. If, however, there has been an abundance of music during the communion rite, singing this prayer could be experienced as excessive.

In conceiving, creating, composing and choreographing the communion rite, ritual artists have much musical potential from which to choose. The principle that "less is more" might well be the aesthetic guide in choosing what and when to sing during these ritual moments.

THE CONCLUDING RITES

Between the communion rite and the concluding rites, parish announcements and episcopal letters, if necessary, are most appropriately presented. This avoids interrupting the ritual rhythm which can readily happen when they are inserted elsewhere. For example, placing these practicalities at the beginning of the liturgy scarcely assists the experiencing of gathering, quieting and opening. It is also unlikely that people will remember facts about the future which are given them just prior to the ritual. Placing them after the homily clearly blocks the felt connection between proclaiming the word and giving thanks to the Lord our God. Ritual language is then overcome by pragmatic talk. Placing them before the prayer after communion severs that prayer from the communion rite which it properly concludes. When the latter mistake is made, the presider often erroneously refers to this prayer as the closing prayer—which it definitely is not!

During the dismissal, the presider greets the people for the final time during the rite. Aesthetically this should be experienced as a brief but climactic moment, not a ho-hum, "thank God we are finished" kind of expression. This can be achieved if the presider sings the greeting, the blessing and the dismissal and the assembly responds to each in song. Mere recitation of the dismissal rite can create a very flat finale.

Then what? Although no music is prescribed in the Roman rite itself for the departure of the ministers and the worshipers, a silent exit ordinarily creates an experience of a deadbeat, flat ending. What is needed is some kind of ritual exclamation point at the end. It is customary, although not officially part of the liturgy, to accompany the departure of ministers and assembly with music, either instrumental, choral or singing by the assembly. If there has been singing after communion, it can be experienced as redundant and musically excessive to invite the assembly to sing a recessional song. After all, they have been told in the dismissal that "the mass is ended" and that they should "go in peace!"

Perhaps those who leave at that time may be more correct ritually than the musicians who ask them to stay to sing. How appropriate is it actually, after the dismissal, for the music minister to say in effect: "Lie! It's not over until its over. That priest has had his final word but we haven't had ours. Please open your hymnals to page 312 and sing all five verses of 'Now Thank We All Our God.' " Many in the assembly don't appear to feel great gratitude for that. They either vote with closed mouths or with their feet by leaving during the song.

Ordinarily the best music for the exit is performed by instruments or by the choral ensemble. This leaves the people free to shift naturally and easily from the formality of a ritual experience and language back into the more casual and informal rhythms of ordinary experience and conversation. It also allows the recessing ministers to look and smile at their fellow-worshipers as they leave. Too often those recessing engage no one with their eyes and faces. Rather they simulate a stiff solemnity and overly-ministerial piety which may make people wonder if they were glad they came!

Part IV

LITURGICAL MINISTRIES

11

Preaching the Word

PREACHING AS A CATHOLIC PROBLEM

"Words, words, words . . . I'm so sick of words. If you're in love, show me . . . show me NOW." Those words of Eliza Doolittle addressed to Professor Henry Higgins in *My Fair Lady* could well be the cry of many Catholics at the end of many a Sunday homily. This is not, however, because they do not want or need homilies. In fact, if you ask Catholics what part of the mass influences them most, what part makes the mass more meaningful and more prayerful, they usually say either the homily or the music. Study after study indicates the value people place upon good preaching. Yet those same studies show that the satisfaction of this need for good preaching is not being sufficiently fulfilled. People more often experience homilies as didactic rather than inspiring, more as statements of doctrine than as life-enlightening utterances.

One reason for this criticism may flow from the fact that we preachers tend to do unto others what was done unto us in our ministerial training. We lecture. We use the words and concepts of human reason to speak to the discursive reason for our hearers. We address the mind thinking. But preachers who are most effective, like Bishop Fulton J. Sheen, communicate more through the use of images, symbols and myths which address the mind imagining. Logic is fine for the classroom but it is not the primary tool for the pulpit. Cardinal Newman said that logic never brought anyone to faith.

This is not, of course, to encourage the irrational. It is to stress the *truth* of aesthetics, an expression of truth which is not contrary to but beyond discursive reason's grasp. In a homily which touches peoples' lives to the point of conversion, the mind imagining more than the mind reasoning must be brought into play. Powerful preachers today understand what John Cardinal Newman meant in the nineteenth century when he said that faith must be credible to the imagination before it can be credible to the intellect. Persons are moved to faith and conversion more by images and symbols than by words and concepts.

Perhaps part of the problem lies with the failure of preachers to understand the theological foundations of preaching. At the time I was becoming interested in the Roman Catholic Church, when I was a Protestant college student in 1954, a priest pointed out to me that Catholics have a great advantage over Protestants. Catholics, he said, have Christ in the sacraments and don't need the preaching that much. All Protestants have, he claimed, is a book and a sermon.

That unbalanced view of the relationship of word and sacrament, of revelation pointing to redemption, has been transcended fortunately by the teachings of Vatican II. Christ is present in both word and sacrament. While this may shock some preachers who rely on sacramental power more than the graced power of the word, this increased appreciation of scripture and preaching is drawn from the deepest wells of Catholic tradition.

Numerous homilies from the patristic period witness to the strong homiletic tradition in the early church. Theology in that time was primarily a reflection upon life experience in the light of the word of God. Justin Martyr, writing about the year 150, says that, after the readings at liturgy, the bishops instructed and exhorted the people to imitate the things they heard. Like the eucharist itself, the bread of God's word was to be broken open, to be applied to the concrete life situations of the people, bringing God's light into the world's darkness. Unfortunately, this theological understanding of preaching as a living application of God's proclaimed word in liturgy weakened during the medieval period, when more didactic and moralistic preaching came to prevail.

Vatican II and subsequent developments have restored the homily as an essential, integral part of worship. *The Decree on the Ministry and Life of Priests,* #4, insists that "the primary duty of priests is the proclamation of the Gospel of God to all." Catholics have usually thought that their priest's primary duty is "saying mass." But the official documents on priesthood indicate otherwise. Even when presiding at sacramental celebrations, the priest is, through the symbolic action of the ritual, making the good news of Jesus present in and for the church and the world.

WHAT IS PREACHING?

A document of the U.S. National Conference of Catholic Bishops, the Study Guide for the Order of Mass, offers a helpful description of the homily. "The homily, an integral part of the liturgy of the word, is a continuation of God's saving message which elicits faith and conversion. It is neither exegesis nor moral exhortation but a joyful proclamation of God's saving deeds in Christ. Basing his preaching on the liturgical texts, the homilist breaks the bread of God's word by actualizing it, by showing how God is continuing to act and speak among his people today. Through the homily the members of the assembly are called to become a holy people so that they can better celebrate the eucharist and offer themselves with and through Christ in the eucharistic prayer."

Exploring the rich meaning of the word "evangelization" can be a helpful way to come to a fresh understanding of the priest's primary responsibility as preacher. Evangelization presents *not truths but a person,* Jesus as enfleshed good news. Such preaching leads people to know Jesus Christ and to experience his presence within, and his unconditional love for all creation. It helps people to get inside him and, better yet, to let him get inside us through the presence of God's Spirit within us. This is quite different from getting to *know about* Jesus as an object of information.

Paul VI's Apostolic Exhortation, *Evangelii Nuntiandi,* states that evangelization is "the essential mission of the church." Believers must help to make Jesus known by the witness of their lives and by their proclamation of the gospel. Witness should always precede proclamation in the ordinary course of making the good news known. This is to be done, not just to make others become Christians, but because this living witness is what Christian life is basically about. We witness and God acts through our witness to convert people to faith in God's time and way.

EN asks what has happened to the energy of the gospel in our day (#4). A partial answer may lie in the fact that the church has been catechizing and theologizing people, including clergy and religious, without having first evangelized them. Our Catholic approach to religious education has explained *about* Jesus but may fail to open persons to *know* the Lord, to allow Jesus' Spirit to come alive within them. It has often been *knowledge about* rather than any *feeling for* the Lord. Our witness and proclamation may not effectively grasp the heart where Jesus can be experienced as good news for life and where conversion begins. Perhaps our concern to "tell the next generation that such is our God," has led us to be primarily concerned with Catholics' intellectual assent to truths about Jesus, rather than first of all opening up people to relate to him in ways which lead to ever-deepening levels of commitment to Christ.

This may sound like an evangelistic, Billy Graham approach to religion. And, indeed, there is a relationship. For Pastor Graham begins his mission in the right place by putting evangelization and personal response to the gospel first before moving people to more fully understand the message catechetically and theologically. Regrettably, his methods may never get into catechesis and theology with his hearers. What may be lacking in his approach is the reasoned catechesis and theology which forms the ground for that personal faith. His approach may also miss the importance of ecclesial structures, i.e., faith communities which can sustain, challenge and critique faith as it develops as part of the individual conversion to Christ.

EN (#15) suggests that the work of evangelization today might well begin with the Catholic people themselves, because they may never have experienced Jesus as good news. Far too many have found our preaching and ecclesial life an experience of "bad news": too rational, too moralistic, too rigid, too legalistic, too impersonal, too patriarchal. Consequently, the faith of many adult Catholics has remained at the level of children. It is too frequently external assent and conformity rather than internal conviction and commitment. As a result many turn away when they can no longer assent to some of the truths which the church teaches. Such adults find it amazing what they can get along without, for their faith was never sufficiently alive within them.

If adults actually experienced Christ's church as good news, would they leave it over a difference of opinion about a moral teaching? Would both Christians and non-Christians see no value in relating to a Christian community, despite its flaws and fractures? Perhaps the old philosophical axiom, *agere sequitur esse* (as a thing is, so it acts), should read today "As someone experiences something, so it becomes for him/her." That is the way many people relate to the church today.

PREACHING AND THE IMAGINATION

Preaching calls Catholics to our "deepest identity" according to EN #2. This papal challenge urges preachers to discover how to more effectively bring persons to know Jesus as Lord in this time, the evening of the twentieth century. Yet many remain puzzled about how to proceed to do this. How does it differ from the ways we have been preaching? How can we preach good news in a fresh way?

The answer calls for a conversion within the minds and hearts of all who strive to make good news known: pastors and parents, teachers and taught. This conversion must be a response to Jesus' initial announcement: "Repent and believe the gospel. The kingdom of God is at hand." Such repentance calls for more than a change of behavior or even a change in attitude or values. It is, before all else, a transformation in the way Christians *see* life: as God's reign breaking into, already present within the world.

The preacher who allows himself to be "turned around" in this way will not see his mission as primarily one of convincing a person's reason or reforming the will. His task is neither principally rational nor volitional. This conversion calls the evangelist to use forms of imagination to appeal to hearers' imaginations. In this way, a new mode-of-being-in-the-world, a way of living which Jesus called the reign of God, can be held out to people. Imagination is a true way of knowing, an authentic cognition which both precedes and transcends reason. Such a mode of proclamation depends for its efficacy upon an epistemology used by Jesus himself. Through parable and myth, through story and symbol, Jesus appealed to the imagination of his followers to see God's gift present in the world.

EN urges just such a revision in our methods of evangelization "with boldness and wisdom" yet with fidelity to content (#40). We are encouraged to borrow ways of knowing from contemporary cultures so that the good news may permeate those cultures (#20). A clue to the direction of this revision: "Man has passed beyond the civilization of the word. . . . Today he lives in the civilization of the image" (#42). Such use of forms of imagination engaging hearers' imaginations can become a fresh way of approaching the age-old mission of evangelization.

The use of imagination in preaching does not mean picture-making or make-believe. It is neither a fantasy escape into the world of the unreal nor is it the "impressed species" of the faculty epistemology of Aristotle/Aquinas. "Fictions do not operate to help us escape reality, but to redescribe our human reality in such disclosive terms that we return to the 'everyday' reoriented to life's real . . . possibilities" (David Tracy, *Blessed Rage for Order,* New York: Seabury Press, 1975, p. 207).

Imagination's forms used in preaching can open up avenues of true cognition by likenessing and comparing. It is the kind of knowing, a change of mental mode, which leads to love, by filling gaps in our knowing which mere words cannot fill, holistic knowing. It is synthetic cognition more than analytical. It grasps truth, not by dividing reality into its multiple, constituent parts, but by opening an avenue into holistic, intuitive cognition.

IMAGINATION IN PREACHING

Preachers need to imitate Jesus who preached that the reign of God is at hand, a kingdom which is both present yet coming in the future. Kierkegaard has said that "we live out of the future and understand out of the past" (Kierkegaard, *op. cit.,* p. 243). The future out of which Christians live is the reign of God. This reality transcends sensory knowledge and reason. It can be grasped best through the imagination. Jesus presented this reign initially by poetic metaphor rather than through concepts and logic. God's rule over all space and time is conceptually inconceivable, although it is not self-contradictory. Through forms of imagination such as image, symbol, parable and ritual acts, Jesus opened up a new mode-of-being-in-the-world which he termed "kingdom"—a commonwealth of love and justice.

Theologian David Tracy speaks of the importance of the imagination in preaching—and in Christian living. "We often find ourselves more deeply transformed and more radically reoriented by such 'supreme fictions' than by the most careful analytic discussion of the distinction between 'is' and 'ought'. To capture how it feels to live a certain way, to provide by that distanciation process we call genre both a proper imaginative entry into and a psychic distance from the 'world' of the novel, film or poem frees us to experience that possibility in all its existential reality. . . . Yet when that possibility is allowed to function as a fiction—a redescription of what reality is and might be—we find that the consequence often includes a reorientation of our own most basic moods, feelings, reactions and actions, our very way of being in this world." The adequacy of this claim for the transformative power of forms of imagination, says Tracy, is common sense. The proof of the pudding is in the eating.

Tracy continues: ". . . human beings need story, symbol, image, myth, and fiction to disclose to their imaginations some genuinely new possibilities for existence; possibilities which conceptual analysis, committed as it is to understanding present actualities, cannot adequately provide . . . by redescribing the authentic possibilities of human existence. . . . Fictions open our minds, our imaginations, our hearts to newly authentic and clearly transformative possible modes-of-being-in-the-world" (David Tracy, pp. 207–208).

Jesus' non-conceptual approach to religious truth is not due simply to his Semitic mentality which tended to "think" in these patterns. It is rather due to the fact that this is the nature of primary religious discourse. The purpose of such language is not obfuscation, ornamentation or information. Rather, it makes possible *participation* in the truth being communicated (John Dominic Crossan, "Parable as Religious and Poetic Experience," *Journal of Religion,* v. 53, no. 3., July, 1973, p. 339). This is the goal of all evangelization and all preaching.

Therefore, whoever wishes to make Jesus known to others, that is, one who evangelizes and preaches, will be most effective when employing forms of imagination. This is what Cardinal Newman meant by the "illative sense." It does not aim at accomplishing what he called "notional assent." This is reason's agreement that subject and predicate agree. Rather, the preacher, using the illative sense, seeks to bring about "real assent" in the hearers by creating imaginal space in which the truth of the message will be disclosed within their own experience.

Vision, the way of seeing the self in all its relationships, can thus be changed, interiorly transformed. In Newman's terms, what is only an antecedent probability in the preached story can thus become really credible in the internal consciousness of the hearer [John Henry Newman, *Grammar of Assent* (New York: Doubleday, 1955), pp. 49–92)]. Newman's illative sense is a function of the imagination. Real assent, an assent that leads to transformative action, involves a decision to act based upon antecedent probabilities and common sense. Through this operation of the illative sense persons come to grasp and be grasped by the truth of faith. As one Newman commentator says, ". . . for an assent to be rationally adequate it must first be credible to the imagination" (John Coulson, p. 14).

THE GOAL OF EVANGELIZATION

In the second epistle of Timothy (1:6 and 14), preachers are told to "stir to flame the gift of God . . . and guard the rich deposit of faith." Imagination is needed in both the stirring and the guarding. As Newman held, people are more moved toward belief by what seizes their imaginations than by what reason grasps. Faith expressed in story form, he contended, preserves truth as ". . . permanent possibilities of experience, besides somehow guaranteeing their integrity as ultimate explanations" (John Coulson, p. 2). Expressions of faith, Newman suggested, develop through the imagination turning around the mystery of Christ until it suddenly clicks into our present awareness. But the click itself will not hold indefinitely. It is variable. Yet what is permanent is preserved in this process.

People and cultures are more deeply motivated by images, mythologies and archetypes than by ideas. Although ideas are fundamental to knowledge, they change more easily than images and symbols. They are not so deeply grounded in the very being of peoples as are the realities expressed through forms of imagination (Amos Wilder, "Theology and Theopoetic II," *Christian Century,* x. XC, no. 44 [December, 1979], p. 1196).

Evangelization calls for such a continuing, lifelong conversion of imagination, heart and mind. It begins with a re-visioning and a re-valuing that over the years reforms behaviors. It reforms life from within in the light of the reign of God, that rule which became human in Jesus and, through the presence of the Spirit, continues to take flesh in the world for those with eyes to see and ears to hear. Could it be that Jesus'power to proclaim his message across cultures and centuries is, from the point of view of the forms of expression used, due to the fact that his religious discourse was imaginative? Could our current lack of gospel energy be partially explained by our concern for conceptual catechesis and theology more than for an imagination-oriented evangelization? Isn't it possible that the new methods called for by *Evangelii Nuntiandi* may be found by pastorally probing various forms of imaginal expressiveness?

Finally, even the use of imagination in preaching will not bring the message home unless the preacher is *a living witness* of gospel truth. The most powerful appeal to the imagination is made by preachers who are living symbols of the Word made flesh. Their embodiment of good news can stir to flame the grace of God with ". . . an interior enthusiasm that nobody and nothing can quench" (EN, Conclusion).

12

Priests: Problem and Solution

Guess whose actions matter most at mass to the members of the assembly—next to the action of God, of course? The *priest* who presides. No one else can so readily make it or break it in ritual. The priest, serving as a kind of conductor of the art of ritual, can unify the other ministers in such a way that, together, they energize the assembly's prayerful celebration. On the other hand, no one else can so thoroughly wreck the rhythm of the ritual and make it seem like a recipe-reading exercise.

Several years ago, when I was serving as director of a diocesan liturgy office, I received the following letter from a frustrated parishioner: "Liturgical abominations abound at our parish so that any communication from your office on liturgical matters is a potential source of frustration for me. Therefore, I must ask that you either remove my name from your mailing list so that I will not continually experience the pain of wounds reopened; or keep my name on the list and promise me you'll remember the reality of St. X's as an example of the powerlessness of the laity and the ineffectiveness of any attempt at liturgical or educational reform in the church unless it first affects the clergy."

Priests' understanding of liturgy both in itself and in its place within the larger life of the faith community; priests' attitude toward communal worship; and priests' bearing within the celebration are both a principal liturgical problem and a major source of the solution to today's liturgical difficulties.

First, *the priests' understanding of liturgy.* Does the priest grasp that liturgy is not just structures and texts to be correctly observed? Does he conceive of ritual as an art form, as something which requires aesthetic rhythms in order to lift the rites off the page into energized celebrations? Does the priest allow an exploration of the various options possible within the approved forms, or does he simply do the same old thing time and time again? Does he consider the liturgy to be the source and summit of the whole Christian life of the faith community, while being aware that the summit is the smallest part of a mountain? In other words, is he aware that life, not just liturgy, is where God acts and that God leads people to the mountain moment of ritual in order to open their eyes to the sometimes veiled vistas of grace breaking through in the valleys of ordinary living?

Here is one example of a failure to understand liturgy. From all of the church's official documents it is clear that the fullest form of sacramental participation involves making available communion under both forms. There are no rubrical limitations on when or on what occasions this may be done. Priests who want the fullest and best participation by their people are moving toward sharing the cup on all possible occasions. Yet many priests have never done so or greatly limit the fullest expression of sacramental communion. This does not, of course, violate the letter of liturgical law, since communion with the bread alone satisfies the minimal requirement for receiving the whole Christ. However, it is an example of a paltry liturgical minimalism which indicates an inadequate understanding of liturgy as an action of grace which causes its supernatural effects by natural signifying. When only one sign of Christ's presence is made available to communicants, less presence is symbolically expressed. Is less caused subjectively for the communicant?

Another example of priests' inadequate understanding of liturgy: The new vernacular liturgy with its flexible moments for priests to say "these or other words" has become both a blessing and a curse. Comprehension and flexibility are the plus. But the increased wordiness of our reformed rituals are the negative side. Multiplying words diminishes the experience of mystery. Too many words, whether in adding to the ritual texts or inventing other words, leads to explanatory and discursive rather than exploratory and imaginal ritual experiences.

For example, some priests have developed the habit of connecting parts of the liturgy with the conjunction, "and": "And the Lord be with you. . . And Lift up your hearts. . . and Let us Pray. . . ." Such verbosity interrupts rather than serves the flow of ritual rhythm. Presiders would do well to recall Matthew 6:7: "In your prayer do not rattle on like the pagans. They think they will win a hearing by the sheer multiplication of words." Words added to ritual texts should be carefully chosen, be more exploratory than explanatory, more poetic than prosaic, more imaginal than rational, and less is most always more. In other words, the priest should choose words which blend into the aesthetic nature of ritual.

Extensive wordiness and chattiness from the presider can have the effect of calling too much attention to himself. Richard Dillon offers caustic criticism and advice on the presider's use of words: "Celebrants usually pursue this goal by filling the already heavy air with gratuitous commentary and bloated paraphrases of the official texts. Not that the sacramentary is a sacred text, nor that less than full advantage should be taken of the opportunities of variation and innovation in the rites themselves; but the style and content of the innovations make a big difference. So often nowadays, style and content seem to divert attention from the proper object of worship to the person and social agenda of him who presides. His introductory remarks, invitations to prayer, homily anecdotes, words of dismissal, etc., all tend to feature the epicentral 'I.' His general intercessions are redolent of political campaign oratory, and the kiss of peace becomes a campaign-swing through the pews! By the time such a celebration is over, worshipers are hard put to recall what Lord they assembled to confess; and they can be excused for not thinking of a Father who knew their needs before they started when a nonstop talk-fest has filled their hour before the altar. Leaders of worship should direct attention away from themselves so as to facilitate access to God, not obstruct it. Their words should be few, and, in view of their instructional function, well chosen. And emblematically, in my opinion, their uses of the first-person pronoun should be restricted to a rigorous minimum" (*Worship,* September, 1985).

Second, *the priests' attitude toward communal worship.* Common pre-conciliar phrases such as "say mass," "read mass," and "offer mass" expressed a particular clerical understanding of what some priests still refer to as "my mass." Such words betray an inappropriately individualistic sense of liturgy and led to the laity's saying "hear" mass. Some still "say mass" facing the people as they did facing the wall: There is very little inclusion of the assembly in the presiders' inviting and greeting enactments and embodiments.

Vatican II envisioned a more inclusive, community experience in which each person is invited and allowed to take his or her full, conscious and active part. It is the entire assembly, not just the priest, which celebrates eucharist. Where more and more members of the assembly are made aware of this by the presider, this vision of communal worship is taking flesh. But this awareness must not be merely *explained* verbally. It needs to be *demonstrated* by the very bodying forth of the presider.

Presiders can fall down on the job on at least two counts in enabling the entire assembly to celebrate eucharist. First, they can invite everyone who wishes to take a ministerial role within and including the worshiping assembly. Yet that invitation is not backed up with either a deepened faith formation or the practical information and skills required for their roles. Second, priests may impose unreasonable limitations on those who may wish to serve. Such happens, for example, when women are not allowed to serve in all of the ministries allowed by current liturgical law. Admittedly the permission to *allow* women to exercise liturgical roles does not *require* pastors to invite women to so serve. However, given to-day's just concerns of women for greater inclusion in church life and in society, priests who willy-nilly choose to exclude women are guilty of injustice and sexist discrimination.

Third, *the priests' bearing within the celebration.* In liturgy, in one sense, what you see is what you get. Its power to stir to flame the gift of God is in its bodying forth, its signification. This is what is meant by the theological expression: sacraments cause grace by signifying the grace being offered in the sacrament. As an action of the continuing incarnation of God's Son, liturgy is embodiment and enactment, not just structured texts to be recited. The way the presider moves, wears the vestments, engages in eye contact with the assembly, uses his facial muscles, speaks and remains silent— all of these are the avenues which open the assembly to the art of ritual. Talking heads read recipes. Priests enact rituals.

Ritual is a species of drama. And all who take part are ritual artists, actors if you will. Their bearing, not just their verbiage, communicates the meaning and makes possible the presence in the sacred rites. As the Vatican's Consilium for the Implementation of the Constitution on the Liturgy wrote in 1968 (tit. 1, no. 11 from *Newsletter,* Bishops' Committee on the Liturgy, June/July, 1983):

> The celebrant's gestures function as signs; they are meant to reveal Christ's presence. But they will be effective as such only to the degree that they are motivated directly by an inner vision, the contemplation of mystery. Careful observance of rubrics, necessary though it is, is not enough here. How can gestures that have become mechanical from habit, sloppy from routine, half-hearted from apathy still function as signs of the work of salvation? The Roman ritual in one text from four and a half centuries ago demanded gestures of celebrants that by their dignity and gravity would serve as an effective message for the faithful, 'making them attentive and lifting them up to the contemplation of heavenly things.' "

Television constantly presents gestures that are beautiful, decorous, and expressive. These screen pictures reflect hours of the most precise training and exacting rehearsal. Should presiders who handle the reality of the new and everlasting covenant not be examples of similar artistic preparations? Such ritual gestures must be learned: bowing, genuflecting, kissing the altar, making the sign of cross, raising the arms in prayer as a gesture distinct from raising the arms in greeting. To be graceful yet simple and unstudied, liturgical gestures demand serious preparation and careful practice. Presiders need to learn by doing what it means to be natural within the formality of the liturgical context. Videotaping, performing before a mirror and the regular feedback of the assembly are helpful means of growing in the art of presiding.

Artistic bearing and gesture take time during the ritual itself. Ritual movement resembles choreography, movement becoming gesture through the embodiment of meaning. Haste, the fear of "wasting time" in ritual, the telescoping of gestures—all of these leave little room for beauty, for the assembly's perception of movement with meaning. On the other hand, an affected slowness that provokes boredom, tedium and possible ridicule must, of course, be avoided. Gracious liturgical gestures need to be shaped both according to the size of the worship space and the size of the presider's body. They should also be adapted to the kind of assembly which celebrates, viz., large or small, formal or informal. Each situation calls for a different kind of embodiment and enactment in the priest's bodily bearing.

The presiding priest within the celebrating assembly is perhaps the most visible, audible sign of the presence of Christ. He bears witness, he symbolizes Christ and the church, to the degree that his bearing, gestures and words allow his own inner contemplation to show through his bodiliness. Thus, "in spirit and truth," the priest turns his gestures into events of grace through which the love of the Father revealed in Jesus Christ will be manifested and diffused through the Holy Spirit.

If priests are to continue growing in their ritual understanding, attitude and bearing, then they must both take for themselves and be given by their people the time required for such adult learning and skill-formation. Since Vatican II, God's people have done quite a "number" on priests. They have become more and more busy *doing* like Martha with consequently less time for contemplative *being* like Mary.

With all of the councils, boards and committees, pastoral ministry has shifted from a mini-monarchical model toward one that is increasingly participative and interactive. But an individual priest can participate effectively in only so much of each group activity. His effectiveness hinges upon his own contemplation of the mystery. In addition there are fewer and fewer priests available and able to do more and more ministry. Although permanent deacons and lay ministers are assuming many ministerial tasks formerly done solely by priests, nevertheless, the more others become involved in ministries, the more the priests seem to be kept busy developing and supporting these expanding ministries.

All of this is said not to make people say "Poor Father! He works so hard!" Not at all! But people who rightly expect a great deal of priests can help them use their time more effectively so that people are well-served and priests can become healthier and holier. This can be done by coming to agreement within the community about what they most need from their priests. What is it priests do which is unique within the community? What does the priest bring that others do not or cannot?

All the baptized are called to be instruments of Jesus who said that he came to bring life more abundantly. But those ordained into ministerial priesthood are full-timed "ordered" to this task within and for the sake of all those baptized into the priestly people of God. How should priests prioritize their time so that their unique contribution to building up the community can become more and more efficacious?

Studies published recently point out that above all else most people want good preaching and good worship from their priests. That presidency of the assembly is what is unique to the ordained. People want spiritual nourishment through their participation in the rituals of faith. Priests are the ones who orchestrate and conduct the ritual channels of interiority. Not that they do it alone. But they are chiefly responsible. As one layperson put it to me, "We want pastors, not proprietors!"

Yet proprietors of properties and hyperactive clerical businessmen is what priests so often become. Such roles are far from the ideals which drew most persons into ordained ministry and so removed from what people most want and need for priests. Others in the community have the gifts for administration, yet priests so easily become sidetracked into becoming proprietors. Why is this?

Several reasons come to mind for why priests find themselves spending so much time on material things rather than spiritual realities. First, some, regrettably, become more comfortable dealing with materialities because they are easier to manage and measure than spiritual growth. In the process, priests give up the personal prayer life which leads to contemplation of the mystery. Such practices makes them go hollow inside and then their *raison d'être* for ministry becomes *doing*. That new *being* in Christ becomes stunted and business is substituted for the search for holiness.

Second, some are plagued with guilt if they do not respond to everyone's call for assistance: groceries when the larder runs out, counseling when the spouse runs out, funding when the money runs out, fixing when the lights go out—and running to the door and phone constantly. A seminary professor once told men preparing for ordained ministry, "You won't necessarily be busy all the time as a priest. You'll just be forever interrupted." Trying to be all things and always available to all people actually serves few people in the ways they primarily need priestly service.

Whether these expectations for busyness are laid upon priests by themselves or by the laity, the effect is a less spiritual presence within the priest and less spirituality from the priest for the people. Wouldn't it be far better if both priests and people agreed that spiritual nourishment is what is principally expected from priests? If this were agreed upon, time could be ordered by those "in Orders" around the central need for prayer, scripture reflection, reading, the arts, general broad reading and the quiet that alone allows the Spirit to merge and mesh within the priest's spirit so that he can give others a drink from that well which is deeper than himself.

It was this same sense of giving priority to prayer and preaching which prompted the first pastors, the apostles, to call others to minister to bodily needs and the temporalities of the community (Acts 6:1–7). As this movement toward shared ministries continues, both priest and people will be happier and become holier— and their liturgical experiences will become better.

Such liturgical improvement will call the community to examine its schedule of liturgies. Too many masses for too few people make for ineffectual presiding and exhausted presiders. The *theology of convenience* tends to triumph over the *theology of community* when it comes to multiplying masses. Because of the obligation to attend mass on Sundays and holy days, parishes have tried to make it easy by scheduling masses on the principle of convenience. But the Vatican II theology of worship as a *community experience* is constantly at war with this older emphasis on making mass convenient for *individuals*. These two operative theologies may not be completely compatible if we become committed to energized eucharistic assembly celebrations on Sundays.

Robert Hovda, with mild but humorous cynicism, notes: "We had long since adjusted ourselves and our view of what it means to be a Christian to the practical realities of urban church life. From branches on a living vine and members of a living body, we had become private and individual clients of an international spiritual corporation. From communities of friendship, prayer and mission, our 'churches' had become buildings spread about to serve us spiritual consumers. So it no longer mattered where I went on Sundays or with whom I gathered. . ." (*Worship,* September, 1984).

The shift back to a more communal sense of worship, not just convenient individual prayer, needs to be taken into account in scheduling liturgies. Convenience cannot be the primary concern. Community must become more and more paramount in determining the numbers and times of the celebrations. Half-empty churches with people scattered like lost sheep throughout cavernous spaces does not facilitate the role of the assembly as co-celebrants. Rather it continues to promote mass as private and obligatory devotion.

Neither does the theology of convenience as determinant of liturgical schedules help priests become more effective presiders and preachers. Too many masses on a weekend can destroy not only priests' effectiveness but it also weakens and mechanicalizes their faith. Fewer celebrations with more people gathered closer together would be a more effective way of developing the awareness and effectiveness of the assembly. Fewer celebrations may make for more genuine celebration, more quality time and energy expended on the part of all—especially the priests.

CLERGY AS PROBLEM

Thomas Day, in his book *Why Catholics Can't Sing: The Culture of Catholicism and the Triumph of Bad Taste* (New York: Crossroad, 1990), blames much of our present liturgical malaise on the clergy. He says: "In the old days, 'the priest' approached the altar with much bowing, breast-beating, and protestations of unworthiness; he left his personality back in the sacristy. 'The people' assembled behind him. Together they offer 'the Mass.' Today, 'the priest' is almost gone. He has been replaced by Mr. Nice Guy, who strides into the sanctuary as the triumphant President of the Assembly. He stands and sits at the architectural climax of the entire building. Everyone's eyes are on him. His face is the center of attention. The celebrant becomes a celebrity. 'The priest' develops a stage character. A star is born" (p. 133). Yes, but . . . !

If ritual is a kind of dramatic action, those who lead are indeed playing a part, an aesthetic role. It is much more than "being yourself." They are not stars of the stage but artists nevertheless, artists of ritual. Here lies, I submit, the core of the current priest-problem in ritual:

1) They are citizens of the United States. As such they are normally neither educated in nor adequately exposed to the arts. Consequently, they have little interest in aesthetic expressions. As males in a highly competitive, even violent society, their aesthetic deficiency is at least doubled. One author paints this painful truth: ". . . our respect for the arts is superficial, for while we pay lip-service to their nobility, in practice we down-grade them to the level of inessentials: things to be indulged in only after the important things in life have been tackled. They are optional extras for the leisured and the cultured; that is the true modern attitude toward the arts" [Tony Birdge, "Cathedral, Worship and the Arts," in James Butterworth, ed., *The Reality of God* (London: Severn House, 1986, p. 173)].

2) Men trained in Roman Catholic seminaries have had their American anti- or a-aesthetic attitudes intensified by a heady intellectual education and individualistic spiritual formation. It has been a preparation for priesthood largely lacking in imagination—one that undermines the contention of Dom Lambert Beauduin that "art indeed is a priesthood" (Douglass Shand Tucci, "The High Mass As Sacred Dance," *Theology Today*, April, 1977, p. 64). In short, American male clerics are formed to be high on reason and law and low on emotions and intuition. With some gratefully notable exceptions, many clergy neither grasp nor are they grasped by that aesthetic cognition which yields insight into truth with feelingfulness. Newman's insight that faith must first be credible to the imagination before it becomes credible to reason is largely missing in seminary formation.

3) Priests are required to be both male and celibate. Although celibacy may, indeed should, give priests the freedom to develop significant intimate relationships with both men and women, the celibate state is for too many, by choice and/or training, an existence without intimacy, without interpersonal love—except for instances with a strong family of origin, one often dominated by maternal ties. The consequence is often a pathetic withering of the capacity for human feeling in priests. Since a rich interior life of human feeling and imagination is developed to a

great degree through experiences of interpersonal intimacy, experiences which lead to the bonding of deep friendships and, for most, the bonds of marriage, some clerics grow cold and sterile in their isolation. For clerics formed to flee friendship and intimacy, that vibrant inner life which can prepare priests for passionate, embodied ritual presiding has been absent. Passionless presiders is the tragic result!

For at least these three reasons it is not surprising that many clerics are inappropriately prepared to lead assemblies in the art of ritual.

THE LARGER PROBLEM: "THE CATHOLIC LOOK"

The priest-problem in liturgy is more than aesthetic, however. The clergy are part of a larger problem of Catholic culture which Day describes as "the triumph of bad taste." If you sit, as priests do, "on the throne," (Day's description of the priest's position within the assembly) one has a unique, bird's-eye view of this Catholic culture in the Sunday assembly. This overview discloses what I call "The Catholic Look." Seeing the assembly's visages might make one think that the limitations of liturgical renewal are principally the assembly's problem.

Many of the people look dulled and dazed of eye. Their body language reflects that of children corralled into obedient, dutiful behavior. The passive resistance to participation on the part of many is palpable. For example, when I move through the Sunday assembly for the sprinkling with blessed water and offer a gentle smile, attempting a friendly-faced interaction with individuals in the assembly (not, I hope, a Mr. Nice Guy, please-love-me look), I am often met with stolid and sometimes hostile glances; that is, if anyone risks looking into my eyes at all. Many simply stare blankly into space. "The Catholic Look" is one of "I challenge you to make me want to be here!" One would not readily say: "See how these Christians love one another." Rather one might remark: "These Roman Catholics look afraid of or disinterested in one another." The experiences of awe and hospitality which are meant to be present are not in great evidence. In fact, feeling and care, as well as mystery, are what appear to be missing in the assembly's ritual.

What could have conditioned this inner attitude and exterior expression of "The Catholic Look" during our liturgies? What cumulative forces over the generations have sculpted, indeed, chiseled those faces? Surely there is no one cause. The problem is multifaceted. One aspect of the difficulty is the relationship between what one experiences in worship and the ways in which the clergy live and move and have their being with their communities, both apart from and within ritual.

CLERICALISM IS PART OF THE PROBLEM

Could it be that "The Catholic Look" has been brought about, in no small measure, by centuries of cultural control of Catholic life by certain types of male celibate clerics? Could it be that their patriarchal bearing and impassive facial expressions in liturgy have conditioned believers not to actively celebrate but to passively observe? Could it be that some of those whom Catholics call "Father" cause people to worship more like children in the presence of a Father-to-be-feared than as equal adults rejoicing in the Spirit that makes all one? "The Catholic Look" resembles duty-being-done under coercion rather than ecstasy in the presence of mystery and joyful sharing of faith with sisters and brothers in the Lord.

Today celibacy unfairly catches the blame for most all of the church's woes. Surely celibacy is not the primary cause of limping liturgies. Yet consider this hypothesis as a piece of the dilemma: isn't it possible that those celibate clerics, whose personal lives may not be significantly touched by deep interpersonal intimacy, are unlikely to facilitate feelingful faith celebrations of God's love which comes in and through other feasts of *human* love? Celibacy lived in obedience as a law rather than as a personal charism and free choice can kill the inner energy which enlivens faith celebrations.

Some clerics may have chosen the celibate life-style as a revered way of serving people in faith. Consciously or unconsciously others may have chosen a life-style in which issues of intimacy and sexuality, indeed the dimension of human love itself, could be simply omitted or avoided in their lives—perhaps out of fear of their own intimacy needs and sexual orientation. In its most negative embodiments, clericalism can allow men to simply play the role and function of priest and thus avoid becoming involved with anyone. This has a devastating impact on liturgies.

Passionless priests presiding over generations of Catholics can have the cumulative effect of creating robot-like ritual behavior and liturgical recipe-reading in assemblies. Such clerical models of stilted or ritualistic behavior *over-against* the people rather than human ritual interaction *with* the people may have drained some of the warm blood of humanity from Roman Catholic assemblies. "The Catholic Look" tends to be a sad look, a passive visage, mirroring perhaps the sadness in the faces of the clerically-conditioned Fathers whose patriarchal presiding can put people in the position of being perpetual children.

These rather severe descriptions of "The Catholic Look" reflect not only what I have too often observed during Roman Catholic liturgies. They flow as well from what I have observed by way of contrast at worship services in several other Christian communities. When I participated in Anglican or Lutheran or Presbyterian liturgies recently, I was aware of a quite different "feel," a remarkably different "look," not that their faith communities do not have their own brands of dysfunction and clericalism.

In those other assemblies, almost everyone picked up the book to sing. Music mattered. The assembly counted. Most actually gave voice to the texts and tunes before their eyes. In the assembly space there was a reverent friendliness, a sense of free expression and an atmosphere of hospitality between members of the assembly and the leaders of worship. There seemed to be a sense among the people that the liturgy belonged to all of them, not just the priest/pastor and the other ministers "up-front." Most looked like they loved doing what they were doing and usually participated with apparent understanding and gusto. To put it in Roman Catholic terms, they looked, felt and sounded like the embodiment and the enactment of "full, active, conscious participation" in worship.

Some may counter that these assemblies have had more years of experience with sung participation. It is more their tradition than ours. They are used to it. Give us time and our people will catch on. Undoubtedly the lack of a tradition of assembly singing *is* part of our problem. But another part of the difficulty lies with those clerics whose impersonal, non-emotional manner of presiding (sometimes never singing themselves!) has set the tone for what is *called* communal action but which in reality is experienced principally as the activity of those up-front folks.

This is not to suggest that such clergy necessarily lack faith or prayerfulness. Many priests, thank God, are men of heroic faith and lead lives profoundly grounded in prayer. Rather it is to say that such interiority may not be sufficiently *embodied* to energize communal celebrations of faith. Our problems with embodied ritual may be linked to the priestly requirement of celibacy, a charism with which many of the ordained may be not gifted.

WILL TODAY'S NEO-CLERICALISM PERPETUATE THE PROBLEM?

The inherited problem of clericalism is just one piece of a much larger problem within Roman Catholicism today. An older, authoritarian Roman Catholic ecclesiology and leadership style is resurfacing. This can create a style of communal interrelating within church life which discourages and even prevents people from feeling like their worship really belongs to them. In the past decade, the Vatican II collegial sense of the church as a *circle* of the baptized, each with their own unique roles and ministries, has shifted backwards. There is retrenchment from the top. Officialdom seems to be trying to shove the inclusive circle back into the shape of a pyramid with clerics at the top and the others praying, paying and obeying at the bottom, feeling the weight of what sits enthroned above.

Regardless of what Vatican II documents say about the entire baptized, priestly people of God sharing responsibility for the life of the church, "The Catholic Look" of many assemblies tends to belie that conciliar vision for too many of our people. Such a semblance of detachment does not reflect community ownership of what goes on either within the worshiping assembly or perhaps even in the rest of the community's life together. The assembly often looks like a group still cowed by the clergy. Twenty-five years of attempts to change that have only made a small dent in the firm armor of "The Catholic Look."

Today a good number of "new" clerics seem committed to putting the armor back in place, to restoring the reign of clericalism over the people of God. Among the growing number of the neo-conservative caste of clerics being ordained in the past few years—both to priesthood and to the episcopacy—there appears to be a fear of sharing "their power" with the laity in general and, in particular, with women religious. Little wonder, since clerical training traditionally leads men not to trust or to be comfortable with lay persons, especially members of the opposite sex. One bishop said recently that he could not imagine sharing his inmost thoughts with a woman spiritual director.

These men often seem aloof from the human condition and reluctant or unable to be part of healthy adult interactions with non-clergy, especially women. In gatherings of the baptized, a great number of the recently-ordained tend to hang together in a corner like frightened chickens when the wolf is around. They do not seem to know how to "be" when they are not up-front and controlling the liturgy. They can appear to be more like functionaries than persons, throwbacks to the weakest pre-Vatican II models of clerical ministry.

Some conservative seminaries and some hierarchical leadership today are emphasizing to these men the messages of yesteryear about the "specialness" of their priestly powers, their difference from others, and their positions of authority. There is concern not to share this superior priestly power with persons in the other various ministries lest their special role as priests be undermined. They fear that their specialness will be lost if they become too close to "the faithful." (Are not clergy also "the faithful?") Isn't this strong concern for being "special" precisely what characterizes the personal problem called narcissism, a problem which psychologists tell us frequently plagues celibate clerics? This driving concern for clerical authority is part of what continues to create "The Catholic Look."

More and more Catholic people, however, are moving beyond this. Since Vatican II they are coming to realize what Eugene Kennedy says: "Healthy religious development demands increasing autonomy, a reshaping and reintegration of one's religious understandings and commitments, so that they are no longer held with the innocent dependent confidence of a child but with the scarred independence of hard-bought wisdom" [Eugene Kennedy, *Tomorrow's Catholics, Yesterday's Church* (New York: Harper and Row, 1988, p. 167)].

PRIESTS AS PART OF THE SOLUTION

If priests are part of the problem, they are also a major part of the solution. To move us beyond "The Catholic Look" we need liturgical leadership which is learning to eschew clericalism. Priest-hood, Yes! Clericalism, No! Let me contrast the two with admitted stereotypes.

Clerics are aloof and apart in their life-style. In groups of the laity they usually move and stand alone. They are authoritarian, pompous, arrogant and at times impudent and insolent. What often appears missing in their lives is the joy and the pain of loving and being loved. They are like automatons speaking in clerical cliques. Consequently love's flipside, namely, power, can become their over-whelming obsession and their way of identifying themselves as persons of esteem. It is this embodiment of clerical power presiding over liturgies and controlling pastoral relationships which contributes toward "The Catholic Look" in liturgy and in life.

Kennedy calls for and senses the collapse of such a clerical style of leadership in the church. An end of this is needed to truly energize our worshiping assemblies. "One familiar and long-revered form of the religious life is now collapsing not because of lack of faith but because its male-dominated structures no longer fit or provide healthy channels for the religious energies of modern women. So, too, the male-bonded culture of clerical life, which is always to be distinguished from the essence of priesthood, is close to ruin, not because of a lack of commitment to ministry, but because its cultural forms are vestiges of the great days of hierarchi-cal preference and privilege, the pre-Copernican inheritance that was spent long ago" (*Ibid.,* pp. 184–185).

Now to describe the priest in contrast to the cleric. Priests who can change the appearance of sad faces in assemblies will be persons passionately and prayerfully alive within a community of faith *and* a community of friends. Such persons need not be males only.

They need to be celibates only. Such persons are described by Kennedy: "A sympathy for the human condition, a readiness to forgive and encourage sinners, a sacramental feeling for the significant junctures of growth, significant relationships, and loss in people's lives: these constitute the elements of spiritual awareness that possesses intrinsic and easily recognizable religious authority. Such attributes define the sacramental sense of the world that must inform and innervate the sacramental ministry of bishops and clergy" (*Ibid.*, p. 169).

It is my suspicion that, where priestly leadership is lacking, Catholics can't sing because they are given little to sing about. On the other hand, the presence of prayerful and vital priests within and among the assembly of God's priestly people may empower, with cumulative effects over the generations, a shift in the culture of Catholicism toward the triumph of good taste in liturgy. . . and in life!

DECLERICALIZING THE CELEBRATION OF EUCHARIST

What would it look like for a non-clerical priest as happily envisioned by Eugene Kennedy to preside with, rather than over, a celebrating liturgical assembly today? Without changing the current structures and texts of the Roman Catholic eucharistic celebration, there are a number of things which can be done by the presider so that it looks, sounds and feels as if the whole assembly is celebrating rather than "Father is reading mass for the children!" Much can be done to diminish the experience of clerical patriarchy even in the present admittedly imperfect rites.

Imagination is all that is required to revision the celebration away from presider-dominance toward baptismal equality. If we are to reimagine the Roman Catholic Church as Archbishop Rembert Weakland has suggested, we would do well to begin with reimagining the role of the presider in the eucharistic celebration. Much of the way our community has been imagined in the past has been cumulatively conditioned over the centuries by a no longer viable patriarchal, clerical domination of the rituals. Let's review the moments of the mass to see what such a reimaginging might mean.

The gathering of the assembly. Presiders can help establish an energy of hospitality and reverence as members of the assembly begin to arrive for the celebration. As people arrive at the church, the one presiding would be with the people, appearing as another believer coming for worship. He or she would best welcome people near the doors of the assembly space, dressed in street clothes rather than liturgical vestments so as not to differentiate himself or herself from his or her baptized brothers and sisters. For this kind of welcoming presence to be possible several things should be avoided during the assemblying time.

(A) The presider should not converse with just a few of the people, but would do well to greet as many as possible. He or she especially should not spend much time with those persons perceived by others to be the most visible and active members of the community. All appearances of "Father's clique" within the community should be scrupulously avoided—even to the point of not paying a great deal of attention to the most active members who, on the other hand, should be informed in advance that they are not being ignored. Better to greet and visit with those least known by all, especially persons who are having difficulties at the time.

(B) The presider should not be involved in the last minute details of arranging the sanctuary and organizing the ministers. Others should do this so that the presider can devote his or her full attention to the arriving worshipers.

The procession. The presider, together with all other ministers in the procession, should sing the processional music along with the assembly. All appearance of "welcoming the celebrant" should be avoided, although this is difficult to do since the one at the end of the procession is symbolically "the most important." This can seem as if everyone has gathered for this grand entry moment. Over the years presiders can come to quite a grand sense of themselves among "the mere faithful" when their "entrance" is so solemnly and formally choreographed.

Another approach to entering, a simpler choreography, could be useful to declericalize the introductory rites. Formal processions from the rear of the worship space actually could be eliminated entirely on many if not most occasions, since it is difficult to avoid the appearance of the arrival of "the Buddha" at the end of the parade. Rather, the entrance could more appropriately symbolize: "Let the greatest among you be as one who serves!"

Who says a solemn entry procession is necessary? The G.I. #25 speaks of the priest and ministers coming in during the entrance song. A procession is mentioned but such an entry could take many forms. It might be best to have all ministers gradually take their places in the worship space, reverencing the altar during the playing/singing of the gathering music. This would avoid the look of the presider and ministers seeming "special," like "the big cheeses" of the community rather than the ones who know themselves to be called to serve, not dominate, the assembly's worship.

The arrangement of the space. "The people of God assembled at Mass possess an organic and hierarchical structure. . . . The general plan of the sacred edifice should be such that in some way it conveys the image of the gathered assembly" (G.I. #257). The assembly's place should allow them to look, sound and feel like *they* are the celebrants of the liturgy, not mere passive participants before whom the ministers perform the rites.

If clericalism—either of the ordained and/or the lay ministers— is to be avoided, the "organic" arrangements for the whole assembly should be emphasized more than the "hierarchical structure" of the worship space without, however, denying the traditional hierarchical ordering of the worshiping community. This involves a careful, balanced emphasis placed upon the assembly without eliminating the distinctive role of the ministers. Since, in the past, we have tended to disturb this balance by overemphasizing the place of the presider, we may need, for a time, to put the emphasis on the other pole to create the experience of the entire assembly celebrating.

But how can the present, traditional spatial arrangements for "sanctuary" and "the places for the faithful" (aren't the presider and ministers also part of the faithful?) symbolize effectively that "the whole assembly celebrates"? How is this possible if the presider and ministers are placed visually and spatially "over against" the assembly like actors on a stage? While it is important that the "distinctive role" of the ministers is visually expressed in the worship space "so that they can readily carry out their appointed functions," all semblance of the specialness, separateness and above-ness of the presider and ministers should be avoided. For as it looks, so it will be!

The G.I. #257 strongly states this concern for a balance between the elements of the ministers and the assembly: "Even though these elements must express a hierarchical arrangement and the diversity of offices, they (the presider and ministers) should at the same time form a complete and organic unity, clearly expressive of the unity of the entire holy people."

The place for the presider within the celebrating assembly needs to be imaginatively reconsidered if the appearances of patriarchal clericalism in the celebration are to be avoided. While, on the one hand, the G.I. #271 states that "anything resembling a throne is to be avoided," on the other hand, it points out that the "priest celebrant's chair ought to stand as a symbol of his office of presiding over the assembly and of directing prayer. Thus, the best place for the chair is at the back of the sanctuary and turned toward the congregation, unless the structure or other circumstances are an obstacle (for example, if too great a distance would interfere with communication between priest and people)."

This brings to mind a story about the first days of post-Vatican II liturgical renewal. Father James Fitzgerald, longtime noble pastor of St. Mark's parish in Peoria, was informed by his two assistants that "the changes" called for an altar facing the people and a presider's chair placed up on the top steps, the predella, of the former high altar. Father "Fritz" was willing to try facing the people at the altar but he balked at the high chair. "I'm not a king!" he said, with the intuitive convictions stemming from his pastoral sensitivities.

I always think of Father "Fitz" when post-conciliar presiders sit enthroned "over" liturgical assemblies. If Roman Catholics are to ever effectively overcome the appearances and experiences of patriarchy and recover from the plague of an aloof clericalism, not only within liturgy but in the lives priests share with the other baptized, priestly people of God, then priests need to be brought down off their "high places" in liturgy and in life. No matter how you cut it, "thrones" is what you get in most current sanctuary arrangements. Could this be a case of what you see is what you get?

Perhaps the G.I. #271 allows for a reconsideration of the

place of the presider and the importance of "the chair" where it suggests that certain structures and circumstances are obstacles to effective leadership of the people of God—in life, not just liturgy. If it is true that "as we act, so we become," then today we need to act symbolically in liturgy in ways that organically unite all of the baptized, priestly people of God rather than in ways that divide them hierarchically. Such a concern would prompt the elimination of a high, central chair for the presider within the sanctuary area.

Where, then, should the presider be located within the celebrating assembly? Two principles can provide useful guidelines.

1. Whenever the presider is leading the prayer of the people or praying in the name of the people, he or she should *stand* in a position which is spatially central within the assembly so that he or she is clearly visible by all and close to, rather than distant from, the worshipers. This would happen during the following ritual moments:

■ *Introductory Rites:* the greeting; the penitential rite; and the opening prayer

■ *Liturgy of the Word:* the gospel; the homily; and the general intercessions.

■ *Preparation of the Gifts and the Altar:* the receiving of and quietly praying with the gifts brought forward by the members of the assembly, making this clearly more a visual than a verbal rite and one which gives more importance to the gifts and the bearers than to the presider. This can be made visible through a choreography which brings the gift-bearers to either side of the presider *at the altar.* The people themselves hold up the bread and wine with the presider's hands under theirs as the blessings are silently or very quietly spoken by the presider. Then the people place the gifts upon the altar, returning to their seats during the washing of hands.

■ *The Eucharistic Prayer.*

■ *The Communion Rite:* the invitation to the Lord's Prayer with the embolism; the peace prayer with the invitation to share the peace of Christ; the invitation to receive the sacrament of Christ's body and blood; and the prayer after communion.

■ *The Concluding Rite.*

2. Whenever the presider is not functioning to direct the prayer, he or she need not be either as visible or as centrally situated in front of the assembly. A seat could be provided at the side of the sanctuary area either separate from or along with any other ministers who would be seated along the sides of the sanctuary area. This would reflect an arrangement common in the Anglican communion. Another alternative, one emphasizing the "organic unity" of the assembly and the equality of all of the baptized, would place the presider and other ministers in the front seats with the assembly except when they are leading the assembly's prayer or fulfilling their proper ministerial functions. This would happen at all moments other than those described above.

The tone of voice. Presiders can dominate more than lead assemblies by both the tone and the pace of their voices. Whenever the presider is addressing the assembly, either praying in the name of the people or inviting the assembly to prayer, he or she should speak in a loud, clear and distinct tone for all to easily hear. Whenever the presider is praying or reciting words together with the assembly, his or her voice, on the one hand, should set the pace and rhythm of the communal prayer while, on the other hand, blending with rather than overwhelming the assembly's words. Presiders can tend to aurally dominate the worship experience through the power of an amplified sound system. This should be avoided whether the presider is praying or singing with the assembly. This would be the case, for example, during the recitation of the Gloria, the Creed, the Lord's Prayer and the Lamb of God.

The pace of communal prayer set by the presider should be neither rushed nor dragged out. A natural rhythm should be established by the presider. Pauses are determined by the cadence of the phrases and sentences, together with the normal need for breathing by the members of the assembly. This is particularly important during dialogical parts of the liturgy. For example, the "Lord, Have Mercy" should be recited with respect for the comma after the word "Lord." There also should be an instant of breath between the repetitions of the litany. The same would be true for the recitation of the general intercessions, and the preface dialogue.

Distinguish primary and secondary. All of the parts of the ritual are not of equal importance. Presiders can diminish their appearance of partiarchal dominance by deemphasizing those secondary parts assigned to them. All of the so-called private prayers of the priest should be said silently and without undue extension of time. Such would include the prayer before the gospel, the presider's words during the presentation of the gifts, and the private prayers during the communion rite. Secondary actions such as the washing of hands should also be done briefly. Anything that resembles clerical magic-behavior is not appropriate in a declericalized liturgy.

The recessional. There is no recessional specifically called for in the Roman rite. A declericalized liturgy might end with the words, "The mass is ended. Go in peace." Then, with jubilant music played or sung by the choir the assembly would simply break up into social conversation and depart informally as each chooses. The presider and ministers would immediately move from their places to mingle with the eucharistic assembly. "We are many parts but all one body."

13

The Liturgy Committee

"Liturgy committees seem to be running out of gas." So say many in pastoral ministry as the last decade of the twentieth century unfolds. Many of those groups, formed in the quarter century since Vatican II, which were responsible for parish liturgical development have dissolved in disappointment. Others fight on in frustration. Yet liturgy committees do have an important role in the worship life of parishes. They just need a new vision of their responsibilities in order to make a fresh start.

Liturgy committees in the past have followed a model of *planning*. Many committees have planned liturgies, recruited and formed liturgical ministers and arranged the worship space. As this model wears thin, another model may well be called for in the present stage of liturgical renewal. This model flows from the growing realization that liturgy is a form of art—the thesis of this book.

Of course, as an act of Christ, liturgy is not so much what we do but what Christ does in and through the community's celebration. It is first and foremost divine action. Yet, on the part of the humans making those signifying acts in which Christ guarantees to be present and active, it is useful to decide just what form of expressive enactment liturgy is. Liturgy is an art.

With the rare exception of the *Yellow River Concerto* composed by a Chinese committee, art is normally not created by committees. A work of art is conceived and created within the integrated imagination of an artist. That may be why "liturgy planning" has reached a dead end. Committee planned liturgies tend to be like a camel—a horse created by a committee . . . lots of humps and bumps and not much flow! Such rituals may lack unity and integrity because they reflect too much of a compromise of the various committee members' desires and tastes.

If liturgies are not planned or created by committees, then who is the creator? The liturgical artist! This is a person who has knowledge of the liturgy as well as some aesthetic sensitivity. It may be the pastor, the religious education coordinator, the organist, the choir director, or anyone else in the community who knows what it takes to lift liturgy off the planned page into an energized celebration. It may be someone specifically hired or trained for this role. Artists can be "made" as well as born!

Just what qualifications are needed? A ritual artist is a person with some aesthetic sensitivity for performance. One must know how to organize the energies of ritual in such a rhythmed, compenetrating way that there is a sense of beginning, development, and completion. This creates a sense of passage, a sense of parts going somewhere, rather than just one darned thing after another. There is a sense of integral flow and rhythm that concludes with a feeling of culmination.

Some parishes may be able to hire someone professionally trained for this role. The salary for such a ritual artist should become just as important a part of the parish budget as religious educators' salaries have become. After all, it is the liturgy which touches most people most often and, potentially, most profoundly. Budgets should reflect that sense of liturgy's priority as "the summit and source of the whole Christian life." It is not the activity which takes most of the people's time. Nor is this where most revenue should be expended. But money allocated for worship needs to become a much higher priority than it has been until now. If money is not available to hire a liturgical artist, then perhaps parishes could share such a trained and salaried person. Or parishes may select one of their own who has some aesthetic propensity and fund the formation and training of that person for the position.

What is the role of the *committee* if the liturgical artist conceives, creates, composes and choreographs the rituals?

First, consider the *job description* for the committee. Its tasks are fivefold: 1) to set policy and select priorities for liturgy under the guidance of the pastor; 2) to choose the liturgical artist who would most competently create celebrations for that particular community; 3) to provide input to the liturgical artist from their current experience and parish celebrations of past years about the seasons being conceived, created, composed, and choreographed; 4) to provide feedback to the artist after the seasonal celebrations have been completed; and 5) to develop programs of continuing education in liturgy for the committee, the liturgical ministers and the parish as a whole.

The latter point is imperative. It is never to be assumed that either the people in the pew or the ministers know all they need to know. Retreats and regular periods of spiritual renewal for ministers are necessary if their ministries are to flow from hearts of faith rather than just become another function to fulfill within a religious club. Liturgical formation includes frequent catechesis about the meaning of liturgy, both in the parish bulletin and woven integrally into the preaching.

Second, consider the *composition* of the committee. All of the ministries should be represented. This means all priests and deacons, the liturgical artist, and representatives of each of the other liturgical ministries: lectors, musicians, ushers, eucharistic ministers, acolytes, those responsible for the worship space, and, finally, a few persons-in-the-pew who have no specific ministry yet who can report on the experienced end-result of the creation of rituals.

Third, consider the *process* to be followed by the committee and the artist. The process follows that of the Four Stages of Creativity for the performing arts of poetry, dance, music and drama. They are taken from Rollo May's book, *The Courage to Create* (New York: W. W. Norton, 1975). Those stages are: 1) Encounter, 2) Expression, 3) Performance, and 4) Perception.

1. *Encounter.* Artists encounter some aspect of the world through both the senses and the imagination. A painter, for example, will spend a good deal of time just looking at a tree, getting a feel for it, before putting brush to canvas. In that intense, interior encounter between the imagination of the artist and the world around him/her, a feelingful insight into the truth of that tree is born. This is more than and other than mere conceptual clarity about the nature of "tree."

With aesthetic insight comes felt commitment. This is one of the differences between scientific and aesthetic knowledge: the feelingfulness of the truth perceived. It is as if the artist had been inside the tree, indeed, had become the tree in a sense, found an inner identity with the tree. This yields insight from inside the tree as opposed to knowledge gained by objective observation from outside. In the same way, the liturgical artist and the committee begin with the encounter. The encounter is dual: with the world of the liturgical texts, and the world today. The imagination of each member of the committee experiences an intense engagement with the texts in tandem with the times in which they are living.

For example, to conceive and create the rituals of the season of Advent/Christmas/Epiphany, the artist and the committee would gather in early fall. They already would have prayed individually with the texts and raised questions about how that word of God is being made flesh today. The fruit of their felt insights into the truth of God's revelation from their individual encounters would be shared.

Images, symbols, myths and rituals which had been significant expressions of the sacred in the past would be trotted out and explored to discover if they have expressive potential for the current times' insight into the truth. New forms will also be suggested as embodiments and enactments of that particular year's imaginative perceptions about the season. How does this season differ from last year's celebrations? What is happening this year which would call for specific modifications of the traditional structures and texts? How can the Spirit engage the imaginations of the people of God this year to facilitate their experience of the reign of God? In this shared encounter, the aesthetic insight is pressed out from the imaginations of the members of the committee as raw data for the liturgical artist's own encounter with texts and times.

The ritual artist participates in the committee experience of encounter, faithfully recording all that is seen and heard. Then he/she goes off into the creating closet and prays to the Father in secret, as any good artist must do. This is the germination, the incubation in which the artist's imagination becomes a crucible forming the many insights into an overarching, integrating aesthetic matrix which will bind the season into one progressive, cumulative celebration. There will be pressed out a rhythmed relationship between the Advent Sundays which will crescendo toward Christmas and climax in Ephiphany.

2. *Expression.* The liturgical artist, out of the active imagination, weaves into a unified whole the external expressions of the matrix. Images, symbols, stories and rituals are integrated into a rhythmed continuum of compenetrating elements. These are recorded on paper and returned to the committee for consideration in mid-fall. They review the artist's work to see if it captured the communal insight about the meanings and feelings of the season for that community that year. After receiving the committee responses, the artist returns to the creating closet to put the finishing touches on the expression. In this way, the artist is not permitted to be a tyrant, dictating a form which is born only of his/her isolated imagination. On the other hand, the committee avoids the pitfall of having created a camel out of too many unintegrated imaginations each having a piece of the action.

3. *Performance.* A work of performed art such as ritual is only halfway "home" when it has been designed on the page. The insights into the truth with feeling must be embodied and enacted. The rituals agreed upon by the committee call for performance by all of the liturgical ministers and the assembly, the performing audience, so to speak. Each of the representatives of the various liturgical ministries must prepare those ministers to perform their specific functions according to the conceived, created, composed and choreographed matrix which holds the cumulative force of the season together. Everyone who performs a role must understand not just the individual function he/she performs, but also the seed, the matrix from which the entire creation will grow.

Some may be nervous about the use of the word "performance" to refer to worship. It may seem phoney, play-acting. Yet, if ritual is a performing art, then it must be enacted, embodied, i.e., performed with competence and, above all, with faith. While it is not theater, ritual is a kind of dramatic action. Only by being faithful to the nature of ritual's aesthetic form can recipe reading be transformed into celebration.

4. *Perception.* In performing the arts of poetry, dance, music and drama, the act of perception takes place primarily in and for the audience watching and listening to the performers. Of course, the performers themselves are also perceiving the unfolding of the art form. Those on stage perform and the audience perceives. But

that is not the case with liturgy. The entire assembly, each in his/ her own way, performs and perceives.

In creating rituals, the liturgical artist and the committee must be extremely careful not to conceive something to be performed up front by the ministers for those out there in the pews. That would return us to the trap of passivity which prevailed prior to the council. In creating the rituals, the assembly must be considered first and foremost as the embodiers and the enactors of the celebration. Their participation will be facilitated if what has been created is fundamentally familiar, i.e., of the family, rather than novel. Structures and texts are to be respected as the nature of ritual is familiar, patterned, repetitive behavior. The freshness builds upon this familiarity.

After the celebrations of a season have been performed/ perceived, the committee and the artist meet for evaluation. Did what we conceive find adequate expression? Were people drawn into the enactments or put off? Was there integrity and rhythm in the rituals? Was there an organic unfolding? Were the ministers properly informed and prepared? What was the overall experience for the assembly?

Based upon what was learned in this creative process the committee, together with its liturgical artist, would meet to begin the process of giving birth to the season of Lent/Easter/Pentecost. In regard to ordinary time, it may be best, unless there are special parish events being celebrated, to create a common, simple, familiar pattern for the celebrations which would be less taxing on all involved. This would also enable the seasons to be experienced as more celebrative because of the freshness and greater intensity of the forms.

One other role can be very useful in the performance/perception of rituals. That is the role of liturgical coordinator. If the liturgical artist serves as the author/creator of the ritual drama, the coordinator is akin to the director and/or producer and/or stage manager of the dramatic action. Such a person would do well to assume such a role for from three to five years. To serve in this role longer may lead to burnout or to becoming something of a controller and tyrant.

A liturgical coordinator should be: 1) a person committed to faith and prayer; 2) a self-starter—one able to work with a minimum of guidance; 3) a wise delegator—one who can use time to manage growth and support people who in turn share the responsibility for the many details; 4) an honest individual—one who can keep communication open with parish staff and liturgical ministers and give honest feedback to *all* of the ministers, including the clergy; 5) a responsible person—one able to follow through or supervise someone else to follow through on necessary details.

In detail, a liturgical coordinator ideally has many of the following qualifications:

Personal
1) Be a fully initiated member of the Roman Catholic Church who participates in the liturgical celebrations of the parish;
2) Have personal skills and abilities for delegating, consulting and teaching and have an interest in personal development;
3) Have a mature spirituality which integrates private, group and liturgical prayer;
4) Have an adequate support system of family, colleagues and/or friends.

Intellectual
1) Have foundational background in at least some of the following areas: liturgy, theology, scripture, spirituality, psychology and education;
2) Have an understanding of the liturgical year;
3) Have a special understanding of eucharistic theology;
4) Have a foundation in principles of prayer.

Organizational
1) Have a written job description which outlines responsibilities, accountability and lines of communication;
2) Have a written description of the relationship with the liturgy committee and the liturgical artist;
3) Organizes, recruits, coordinates, evaluates liturgical ministers and integrates new members on a regular basis;
4) Evaluates all phases of parish liturgy to assure growth based upon clear assessment of needs in conjunction with the pastoral staff and the liturgy committee.

14

Music and Musicians

THE VISION

"Musical liturgy is normative." This phrase has been popular since Vatican II's Constitution on the Sacred Liturgy (1963): ". . . sacred song united to the words. . . forms a necessary or integral part of the solemn liturgy" (#112). "Liturgical worship is given a more noble form when the divine offices are celebrated in song . . ." (113).

The same emphasis is expressed in the U.S. Bishops' Committee on the Liturgy document, *Music in Catholic Worship* (1972): "Among the many signs and symbols used by the Church to celebrate its faith, music is of preeminent importance" (#23). Music heightens the meaning of the texts, adds joy and enthusiasm to the celebration, and unites the assembly in the mode and mood of the particular celebration. "Music, in addition to expressing texts, can also unveil a dimension of meaning and feeling, a communication of ideas and intuitions which words alone cannot yield. This dimension is integral to the human personality and to man's [sic] growth in faith. It cannot be ignored if the signs of worship are to speak to the whole person (#24).

Kevin W. Irwin sums up the power of arts such as music when used in liturgy: "The issue in liturgy is less verbal understanding and mental comprehension by the mind and more a shaping of attitudes and allowing one's imagination to be engaged in symbolic acts, which by their nature are not oriented to comprehension alone" (cited in Thomas Day, *Why Catholics Can't Sing: The Culture of Catholicism and the Triumph of Bad Taste,* New York: Crossroads, 1990, p. 113).

The intrinsic importance of music in worship was reiterated in the same episcopal committee's subsequent document, *Liturgical Music Today* (1982) which describes liturgy as "inherently musical" and a "necessarily normal dimension" of all Catholic worship. A positive assessment of music in worship was offered. "Liturgical music today exhibits signs of great vitality and creativity. . . . The ministerial role of liturgical music has received growing acceptance and greater appreciation by the Christian people. The sung prayer of our assemblies, often timid and weak but a few years ago, has taken on the characteristics of confidence and strength. In the liturgical ministry of music, more and more capable persons are assuming roles of leadership. . . . New musical compositions are appearing in great numbers and the quality of their craftsmanship and beauty is improving. All these developments serve as signs of hope for the present and future of liturgical music" (#1).

MUSIC AS PARADIGM FOR RITUAL

Music, well-crafted, carefully chosen and competently performed, can indeed bring heightened vitality to the assembly in liturgy. Music, more than any of the other liturgy-related arts, prepares hearts to experience the Lord's presence in ritual. Someone once said to me, "Music makes the mass!" Theologically, of course, I had to disagree. The action of God in Christ makes the mass. But experientially, I said, "Right on!" Peoples' experience of God's action and their openness to that divine power are profoundly enhanced by those ordered sounds-in-motion called music. Our experience of God's word and sacrament are heightened and intensified when music captures the ritual moments' inner dynamism, color, feeling, and meaning. If you doubt this, just try reciting "Ave Maria" and then listen to Franz Schubert's sung setting. Music MAKES it, doesn't it?

As Aaron Copland wrote: "It is the very nature of music to give us the distillation of sentiment, the essence of experience transfused and heightened and expressed in such fashion that we may contemplate it at the same time we are swayed by it" (Aaron Copland, *Music and Imagination,* Cambridge, Mass.: Harvard University Press, 1952, p. 10).

Ritual music can transform the ordinary experiences of life

that participants bring to the celebration. It can intensify and deepen people's engagement in reality, giving their lives new meanings, values and directions. In such experiences participants do not merely *observe* the moments of life, they enter into those experiences with deeper *participation* in them. Participants can be moved from life as a landscape to the *inscape* of life, from observation to perception, from random experiences to a life of inspired, defined events.

All of this can happen through imagination being engaged by the sounding forms in motion of music. In ritual the imagination is triggered by music to discover meanings in human experiences, meanings which transcend the senses and discursive reason. For example, I sang Schubert's "Ave Maria" during a retreat for retired priests. One man told me, "That was my whole retreat!" It had drawn forth memories of fifty-six years of priestly ministry—people, events, joys, sorrows. Imagination stirred within him and put together those memories into a new constellation of present presence for him. The truth of his life was experienced afresh with emotional engagement and in a way which unified his life experience as priest.

Copland again: ". . . it is the imagination and the imagination alone that has the power of balancing the combined impressions made by themes, rhythms, tone colors, harmonies, textures, dynamics, developments, contrasts" (Copland, p. 15). Through the mind acting as an imaginative knowing power, the reality of the ordinary dissolves, diffuses and is re-created. Persons see anew what their experience means. Music, as the art which is most woven into the art of ritual, has perhaps the most pervasive power to bring about this transformation. Music is an instrument of God's grace.

What happens in musical composition is analogous to what happens in the liturgical artist's conception, creation, composition and choreographing of ritual. In both musical and ritual composition, the first stage is the conception. A germ motif is perceived as the ritual artist/composer of a worship service prays with the ritual and scriptural texts, relating them to the present experience of that particular worshiping community. In silence and solitude, in prayerfulness with the Spirit, a dialectic between word and life takes place in the "composer's" intuition. From this creative intuited tension, the commanding form of the whole worship-art-work becomes present in embryo. The matrix of the work has been disclosed in and to the imagination.

The next task is to organize the energies of ritual, namely, words (like poetry), sounds/silence (like music), movements/gestures (like dance), and action (like drama). The seed, from these organized energies, begins to give birth to the expressive form of the liturgy. The principal problem becomes ". . . how to extend successfully the seminal ideas and how to shape the whole so that it adds up to a rounded experience" (Copland, p. 43). Under the influence of the germ motif, every part of the piece is composed into an organic, unified ritual. As art philosopher, Susanne Langer, wrote: "The essence of all composition . . . is the semblance of *organic* movement, the illusion of an indivisible whole" (Susanne K. Langer, *Feeling and Form*, New York: Charles Scribner's Sons, 1953, p. 126).

THE RHYTHM OF RITUAL

This organic organization of energies is precisely what musicians know and feel as *rhythm*. Rhythm energizes ritual celebrations. Just what is rhythm? "The essence of rhythm is the preparation of a new event by the ending of a previous one. . . . Rhythm is the setting-up of new tensions by the resolution of former ones. . . . the situation that begets the new crisis must be inherent in the denouement of its forerunner" (Langer, p. 127).

For ritual to be a moving, rather than a boring experience, a feeling for ritual rhythm from moment to moment is crucial. Each moment flows from the last and sets up the next. Something happens to the sense of time in ritual which is comparable to a musical experience of time. "Music makes time audible, and its form and continuity sensible" (Langer, p. 110). Ordinary time is suspended and the illusion of imaginary time, perhaps eternity, is created. It is not time as a mere succession of moments, time as pure sequence. It is time transformed into an expression/experience of *passage*.

What is meant by passage? Langer wrote: "The primary illusion of music is the sonorous image of passage, abstracted from

actuality to become free and plastic and entirely perceptible"
(Langer, p. 113). By means of such passage, participants in ritual
step out of ordinary time briefly, passing through eternity made
sacramentally visible, in order to return to their experience renewed in vision and values.

This movement, this rhythmed time, is created in music by
tensions and resolutions building to a climax and subsiding. The
same rhythmic sensitivity can energize ritual time. If one can create and perceive music's rhythmic dynamisms, its rise and fall,
then one can, out of the same intuitive creativity, both create and
participate in moving rituals.

Both music and ritual as expressive forms are performing or
occurrent arts. They occur, they happen, they grow ". . . from the
first imagination of its general movement to its complete, physical
presentation, its *occurrence*" (Langer, p. 121). This, in all its details, both in music and liturgy, is the work of artistic imagination,
creating and developing ". . . the illusion of planning time in its
passage, an audible passage filled with motion that is just as illu-
sory as the time it is measuring" (Langer, p 120). Through this
perception of ritual rhythms, participants can become caught up in
the experience, knowing through aesthetic perception a secret but
disclosed mystery.

John Dewey, in *Art as Experience,* expresses similar ideas
about the cumulative effects of rhythm in art. It ". . . will be serial
in order to grasp the whole and each sequential act builds up and
reenforces what went before" (John Dewey, *Art as Experience,* p.
136). This is precisely what it means to create and perform
rhythmed ritual. Dewey elaborates this insight: "There can be no
movement toward a consummating close unless there is a progressive massing of values, a cumulative effect. This result cannot exist
without conservation of the import of what has gone before. More-
over, to secure the needed continuity, the accumulated experience
must be such as to create suspense and anticipation of resolution.
Accumulation is at the same time preparation, as with each phase
of the growth of a living embryo. Only that which is carried on is
that which is led up to; otherwise there is arrest and break. For this
reason, consummation is relative; instead of occurring once for all
at a given point, it is recurrent. The final end is anticipated by

rhythmic pauses, while that end is final only in an external way" (Dewey, pp. 137–138.)

In both music and ritual, then, rhythm is not the equal division of time. It is not simply one movement following another without felt relations. This leads to boredom and obsessive, compulsive ritual behavior. Rhythm is, rather, a relationship between tensions. It is the energy which happens "between the downbeats." "Everything that prepares a future creates rhythm; everything that begets or intensifies expectation, including the expectation of sheer continuity, prepares the future . . . and everything that fulfills the promised future, in ways foreseen or unforeseen, articulates the symbol of feeling" (Langer, *op. cit.*, p. 129). This is the felt awareness of the presence of mystery.

Such rhythm in music and in ritual is what creates the expression and experience of aesthetic feeling for participants, not brute emotion but aesthetic feeling. Isn't it such feeling that believers long for in worship? Is it not a feeling of God's transforming presence that we expect when we assemble to celebrate faith? Music organizes our *conception* of feeling so that it is more than an occasional awareness of emotive storm. So does liturgy. Both create the possibility of insight into feeling and into faith. In this way our experiences of life become more unified, more complete, and more a greater awareness of the reign of God which is present *in* but not *of* this world.

Sharing in these aesthetic qualities of art opens up for participants a deeper sense of the significance of their lives. What is presented is a sense of human feeling as ". . . a complex experience that moves and changes" (Bennett Reimer, *A Philosophy of Music Education*, Englewood, Cliffs, New Jersey: Prentice-Hall, 1970, p. 36). Participants receive not just *information* about feeling but an *experience* of feeling, one that is intensified, unified, and transformed. A knowledge of "how feelings go" is communicated and participants' visions are changed. The worshiper can become new through cumulative participation in liturgies. Of course no one liturgy and not all liturgies can be expected to be the fullest experience of the transforming mystery.

Once again, those who create the art of ritual would do well to learn from those who create musical arts, both composers and performers. Both ritual and musical artists become deeply involved with the medium in order to explore and capture its expressive potential. "As an artist 'works out' the expressive possibilities of his medium he is at once embodying his understanding about the nature of feeling and exploring new possibilities of feeling. The thing he creates contains his insights into subjectivity, capturing both what he brought as person to the act of creation and what he discovered during that particular act of creation. . . ." (Reimer, p. 49; one apologizes for the lack of inclusive language in this quotation.)

PARTICIPANTS AS ARTISTS OF RITUAL

Those who participate in the art of ritual experience the aesthetic qualities created. They, too, come to share the ritual artist's insights into subjective, felt reality which have been captured in the ritual forms. The participant discovers his/her own unique meanings from that experience. Both a sharing and a discovery takes place. "In this sense it is also a creative experience, in that new insights into feeling are made possible as he [sic] grasps more and more of the work's expressive subtleties" (Reimer, p. 49).

In the composed liturgy as in the musical composition, participants are not simply given a product to observe. They are invited into an imaginative process along with those who created and those who ministerially lead the performance of the work. The art works its power within the imagination of the perceiver/participant, shaping his/her experience by the shape of its expressive content. But the participant must, at the same time, create his/her own experience of spirit merging and meshing with Spirit through surrendering to the embodiment and enactment of the ritual. That is full, active and conscious participation in the fullest sense.

Such interior participation is an imaginative and emotional perception of the aesthetic, expressive qualities of the performed ritual art. The participant becomes absorbed in liturgy's expressive powers. One could say of liturgical participation what Bennett Reimer says of musical perception: "The experience is marked by an absorption in the way the music sets up expectations, deviates from expected resolutions, causes uncertainty in modes of continuation, delays expected consequences of events, satisfies musical implications" (Reimer, p. 99).

Both music and ritual then open up avenues into spiritual experience. Copland says: "What happens is that a masterwork awakens in us reactions of a spiritual order that are already in us, only waiting to be aroused" (Copland, *op. cit.,* p. 17). Such a phrase is reminiscent of the traditional Christian insight: human nature is suffused with grace, only waiting to be aroused by experiences that put persons deeply in touch with that core of themselves which is mystery.

THE VISION IMPEDED?

But the ideal of music in ritual is far from realized in many contemporary liturgies. Complaints about the state of music in worship abound. Some worshipers simply don't like to sing. Others judge the new ritual music jejune, banal and destructive of the experience of mystery. For example, in a January 19, 1986, column in the *Peoria Journal Star,* a Catholic arts critic and parish musician, Jerry Klein, leveled serious complaints at liturgical music and church musicians. He moaned that "the music has become so bland and so trivial that it does not inspire reverence, mystery, devotion or even joy, but at least in some people I know, a stony resentment."

Compared to what he recalled from the masses of yesteryear, such as "Trappist monks chanting their Matins and Lauds," today's church music "approaches the disgraceful." It "has the feel of upbeat Muzak for the masses," performed on tinny pianos, guitars, and drums. And it is played by people "waving their arms and clapping their hands like a group of wild aborigines at a fertility rite." Others, such as Thomas Day in *Why Catholics Can't Sing: The Culture of Catholicism and the Triumph of Bad Taste,* have echoed and doubled the decibels of these unhappy complaints.

Yes, BUT. . . !

Yes, a good deal of new liturgical music is of poor quality. Ray Repp, a friend who composed the early-on popular song, "Here We Are Altogether As We Sing Our Song," confessed to me some years ago his embarrassment about this early work. Yet he pointed out that this effort was composed for his seminary class. It was not initially intended for wide dissemination. The fact that this in-house music became so instantly popular all over our land signified that so little, except solid Protestant chorales, was available to us when we began the assembly's sung participation after the council.

But it took hundreds of years to develop the great Gregorian chants and the literature of Palestrina, the departure of which Klein laments. Don't we have to be patient? Some music of much higher quality for congregational and choral participation, in several idioms, is now being published. Time will eliminate the weeds from the wheat!

Yes, those whom Klein calls "progressives" may have "cast out the church's mysteries and its treasure and have scorned its rich history of music in favor of the banal and the stupid."

But, just when and where were Gregorian chants and Renaissance polyphony actually performed in our nation before Vatican II anyway, outside of some monasteries and great cathedrals? And, even in parishes where these treasures were performed, were they properly rendered? No! In most cases, accurate memory would say "Not often" and "Often poorly."

Klein suggested, possibly with selective memory, that folks his age (in their sixties now) have "lived through the time when the ritual and liturgy of the church were at their fullest flower. . . ." Yet, in reality, before Vatican II we usually listened to saccharine hymns equally as "banal, stupid and disgraceful" (to quote Klein) as some of the "Run, Jane, Run" music inflicted on us in the last quarter of a century. A close reading of liturgical history suggests that our worship has yet to be in "fullest flower" and that it is in constant need of reform, renewal and inculturation.

Yes, in far too many parishes, as Klein observed, "community has become more important than worship, and commonness more the norm that respect. The liturgy has evolved into such an ordinary, everyday experience that people no longer feel compelled to dress up." Agreed, the flip casualness with which too many liturgists and worshipers approach the sacred mysteries is surely one of the most serious failures of the Vatican II renewal.

But should the corrective solution be a return to silent spectators watching a priest pray in a foreign tongue facing the wall with a choir of debatable musical competence performing alone behind everyone's backs? I think not.

Even though there have been gross post-conciliar misinterpretations of what "community" means in worship, the rituals of the church are essentially communal. They are neither private affairs nor gatherings of the like-minded even though many "progressives" have, at times, perverted "community" by defining it largely as a matter of warm fuzzy feelings rather than the gathering-into-one of the scattered children of God. Even though good liturgy has little to do with "how I feel about that," Catholic worship still must be "down to the people" (to quote Klein again) and involve the active participation of each person according to his/her proper role.

Yes, liturgy is of the people, by the people and for the people. But "down to the people" need not mean making the assembly either monks or Muzakers.

Those responsible for parish worship and music take their ministries more and more seriously. By this I mean several specific things. This means hiring or training competent church musicians and purchasing quality instruments. This means purchasing the best of the new congregational/choral music and weeding out the tripe with which we have become comfortable since Vatican II. This means musicians should become familiar with the best of ecumenical Christianity's rich treasure of sacred music. Much of the best of the past is not beyond the musical reach of the average parish assembly and music ministry. Finally, this means that musicians must never forget that their performance is prayer, not the swinging and swaying of a rock group or the self-conscious performance of a concert choir.

So, "Yes, But. . . !" is one dialogical response to my good friend, Jerry Klein, and to others who bemoan rightly their negative experiences of some current liturgical music. Their "yes," I believe, is true as far as it goes. But the "but" is the other half of the story. I sympathize with what is obviously a great sense of personal loss and pain for those who are dissatisfied. Having been trained myself in Gregorian chant by Dom Joseph Gajard of Solesmes Abbey, and being a professionally trained classical musician, I too regret that more of the *patrimonium musicae sacrae* is

not being used in rituals today. Yet I believe that the future can
never be a mere repetition of the past. The future will body forth
from coming generations of musical and liturgical experiences
through the turn of the century and beyond.

SINGING *AT* MASS OR SINGING *THE* MASS?

Musical liturgy may be normative. Ritual music may be improving. But still many Catholic people stand with arms folded,
looking like the stone over the tomb on Good Friday when the
assembly sings. A friend was singing with gusto the "Holy, Holy,
Holy" at mass one Sunday when she heard a man behind her, in a
stage whisper, tell his wife: "If that woman likes to sing so much,
why doesn't she join the choir?"

According to the Notre Dame Parish Study, in observing sev-
enty masses in thirty-six parishes across the United States, 13% of
these "celebrations" had no music at all. 51% had music but no
accompaniment, 62% had no cantor, 60% had no choir or musical
group to lead the congregation. Yet 9 out of 10 masses did have
some singing, ranging from 70% at Saturday evening celebrations
and 90% on Sundays.

All are meant to sing, not just those who have good voices
and/or enjoy the musical experience. Why, after a quarter of a
century, do so many Catholics still dig their heals in and resist sung
participation? And why is music still not greatly emphasized in
parish liturgies? A parallel case: when people attend a birthday
party and the cake with glowing candles is presented, everyone,
good voices and not so good, bursts into song: "Happy Birthday to
you. . . ." Not even the one who sings like a frog would be comfortable being silent. Not to sing, not to participate, is to fail to show
love to the one being honored.

Why do people sing in that kind of celebration? First, all sing
because it is expected. It would be out of place to remain silent.
Second, all sing because they have a common reason for being
there. Someone they care about is the focus of celebration. Third,
all sing because the song is familiar, indeed, it is a traditional ritual
song. Fourth, all sing because, for the most part, the folks present
know one another, at least to some extent. There is an ease in that

assembly. Fifth, the size of the group is probably both large enough to make a solid sound yet small enough so that everyone can be near one another and support one another in song. To sum up, folks sing at birthday parties because it is truly right and good to do so—and it works.

How do we transfer those birthday ritual insights into our liturgies? The same elements that make birthday singing work can apply to *singing the mass.*

First, folks need to be told, again and again, that song is an integral, essential part of their active participation. This can never be said enough—in homilies, instructions, bulletin announcements, parish missions and retreats—with gentleness and respect, with relentless firm courage, and also with humor.

Second, members of the assembly need a common reason to be present. That needs to be a reason stronger than fulfilling the Sunday obligation. The more the members of the assembly are aware of a personal desire to give thanks and praise to God, the more the singing will be effective. A religion of duty needs to be replaced with a spirituality of conscious creativity. Legal observances do not celebrations make.

Third, musicians need to give assemblies enough simple and familiar refrains and acclamations that the singing can be largely spontaneous. Too much unfamiliar music leads to a silent assembly. The structure of the liturgy itself indicates the parts to be sung. "The first place to look for guidance in the use and choice of music is the rite itself" (*Liturgical Music Today,* #8).

Fourth, folks sing better when they are in close proximity to one another than when they are scattered about a large worship space. Knowing one another also is useful. Closeness, both spatial and interpersonal, encourages singing. We may need to adjust the size and shape of our spaces for liturgy in order to bring the members of the assembly into a closer relationship to the ambo, altar and one another. It may also be important to look at the number of masses celebrated in the parish. If only a few are present at a mass, perhaps consideration should be given to consolidating mass schedules. Let the theology of community become stronger than the theology of convenience!

Some thoughts on improving the singing of the assembly:

First, what is sung makes a big difference. There is a major difference between liturgical or ritual music and religious music in the broader sense. A question to ask: Do you "sing *the* mass" or do you "sing *at* mass"? Those assemblies which regularly sing the parts of the mass which are, by nature, musical, tend to sing better than those which concentrate on a large variety of hymnody and religious songs.

Folks become familiar with the Alleluia melody, the eucharistic acclamations, and the litanies of the Lord, Have Mercy and the Lamb of God. These are innately musical moments and are at their best when sung rather than recited. This is what is meant by "singing *the* mass." The opposite, "sing *at* mass" or "singing *during* mass," emphasizes the frequently changing music of the processional chants. This produces less effective results from the assembly and puts the ritual emphasis in the wrong places.

"Singing at/during mass" is what has been called the four-hymn syndrome: the four hymns/songs for the procession, the preparation of gifts, the communion and the recessional. This is regrettable because it establishes an improper rhythm in the ritual The rhythm is backwards. Since singing heightens and intensifies ritual moments, such an emphasis puts weight on the secondary moments of the rite. It accentuates the secondary parts while leaving the primary parts as lowered, recited experiences. "Singing *at* mass" language needs to be replaced by the phrase "singing *the* mass."

The structure of the rite gives the best guidance about what should be sung. Singing according to "the structure of the liturgical unit" means, for example, giving primary emphasis to the musical units within the liturgy of the word: the responsorial psalm, the gospel acclamation, ". . . and sometimes an acclamation after the homily or profession of faith" (*Liturgical Music Today,* #7). Singing during the entrance rite is secondary to the music of the liturgy of the word. Within the liturgy of the eucharist, primary musical emphasis would be placed upon the eucharistic acclamations and the Lamb of God.

Second, the accompaniment can make or break the assembly's song. "The song achieves much of its vitality from the rhythm and harmony of its accompaniment. Instrumental accompaniment is a great support to an assembly in learning new music and in giving full voice to its prayer and praise in worship" (*Liturgical Music Today,* #57).

A good instrument and a well-trained liturgical musician are essential. All too often the electronic organs and tubby old untuned pipe organs in even our finest parishes lack sufficient brightness to encourage and lead the singing of the assembly. Still, even a fine pipe organ cannot sustain singing if the organist uses the wrong registration, fails to keep a steady tempo, or fails to "breathe" with the singers. The Notre Dame Parish Study disclosed that assembly singing is more likely to be wholehearted when the organ is played throughout the liturgy than when a guitar is played. When a guitar is used, people at the front sing well, but people at the back sing less, if at all; the organ generally achieves more uniform participation.

Third, the quality and style of the music makes a difference. The Notre Dame Study shows that in most parishes hymns and folk music rather than the more desirable ritual music predominate. "In terms of their effectiveness in involving the congregation, hymns are above average, but they do even better in celebrations where they are used but do not dominate the celebration. Folk music, it must be admitted, emerges with very mixed results. Often it is associated with very enthusiastic participation, but the participation is by a limited part of the congregation; equally often, the congregation appears quite unresponsive."

Fourth, vocal musical ensembles can be but are not always helpful. They both support the singing of the assembly and add their own unique beauty to the ritual. But many choirs find themselves confused today. A choir director friend was beside me at a dinner party. "Do we still really need choirs in the new liturgy?" she asked. She explained her frustrations with her ensemble. Some resist any special choral music saying that the assembly is supposed to sing everything. They quit singing in the choir and become singing members of the assembly. Others want more choral music because "those folks in the pews don't sing very well anyway." They become frustrated with the small quantity of music expected of them as well as what they sense to be the poor quality of some of the new choral repertoire.

The *Constitution on the Sacred Liturgy* (#114) states that choirs are not to be abandoned as the whole body of the faithful takes up its own active sung participation. On the contrary, "choirs are to be diligently promoted." First of all, choirs are needed to lead and support the singing of the assembly. Second, they can add their own unique beauty by singing alone at appropriate moments. Their role is both/and, not either/or.

The danger of choirs in liturgy is, of course, that the choir can dominate the assembly. Even though this may not be the choirs' intentions, assemblies can sit back and take it easy when choirs seem to be doing the musical work. All liturgical ministers must promote the assembly's song goals" (*Liturgical Music Today* #66).

Choirs can add great beauty and solemnity to the ritual when they perform alone. Choirs can effectively sing alone as a choral prelude or choral invitatory before the procession, a song at the preparation of gifts on some occasions, music during the distribution of communion, the Gloria on special occasions, and during the recessional. In addition, choirs can enhance the assembly's melodies by singing in harmony or adding a descant to the melody. To do this well—to do this in a way that is pleasing both to the assembly and satisfying for the choir—to do this as sung prayer—all this takes time, talent, training and commitment. It also takes money in parish budgets allocated for liturgical music and musicians. "The musicians' gifts must be recognized as a valued part of the pastoral effort, and for which proper compensation must be made" (*Liturgical Music Today,* #66).

Indeed, the entire assembly celebrates a musical ministry, according to *Liturgical Music Today* (#63). But gifted and trained musicians are essential leaders of the assembly's musical worship. As *Liturgical Music Today* states: "Thus the pastoral musician is not merely an employee or volunteer. He or she is a minister, someone who shares faith, serves the community, and expresses the love of God and neighbor through music" (#64).

In particular, the developing role of the cantor is stressed as one "having a crucial role in the development of congregational singing. Besides being qualified to lead singing, he or she must have the skills to introduce and teach new music, and to encourage the assembly. This must be done with sensitivity so that the cantor does not intrude on the communal prayer or become manipulative. Introductions and announcements should be brief and avoid a homiletic style" (#68). "The cantor's role is distinct from that of the psalmist, whose ministry is the singing of the verses of the responsorial psalm and communion psalm. Frequently the two roles will be combined in one person" (#69).

PRIESTS AND MUSICIANS

In my work in liturgy over the years I often had occasion to be with the two groups of persons whose gifts and vocations are essential for the church's life of worship and prayer: priests and musicians. Since I am both a priest and a musician, I find myself frequently straddling the fence when talking with one group or the other. Such a posture makes one liable to injury!

Every time I am with a group of liturgical musicians I hear the same complaint about us priests: "Why aren't they at this workshop or class to learn these things too?" And I must admit, in the courses I teach and the lectures and workshops I give, my brother priests and deacons are regrettably notable by their absence.

When I describe to musicians that Catholic ritual is enactment and embodiment, they will chant: "Right on! Alleluia!" But then comes the sad look in their eyes. "But our priests don't see it this way. They seem to prefer to just wing it, to read the recipe"; Or, "My pastor just wouldn't know how to do liturgy as an art even if he believed it." Or, "How can we ever get the clergy to understand?" What can I say?

Sometimes I have observed a marvelous common understanding between priests and musicians. They know that they must do more than read the words and sing the songs if the assembly is to be helped to experience the presence of mystery. In other situations, however, divisive understandings of the nature of ritual create a frustrating stand-off between these two key groups of liturgical leaders.

On the other hand, many times when I am with a group of priests I hear complaints about their liturgical musicians. Some grumble about their unrealistic expectations for the clergy and for liturgy as well. Others judge their musicians may know music (although some question even that) but they don't understand how music should enliven the rhythm of ritual. Still other musicians are simply strung-out and exhausted by the many diverse and sometimes contradictory demands made upon them in their pastoral duties. They just cannot attend every meeting, conference and lecture which their pastors think they should. But just what should musicians do in order to become more effective in their ministry—and better collaborators with the priests?

From my fence-straddling position—with an ear turned to each side—it seems to me that the first step toward ending the complaints and frustrations involves open communication between priests and musicians—less talking *about* and more talking *with!* Perhaps they should discuss and pray together Matthew 18:15–17: "If your brother should commit some wrong against you, go and point out his fault, but keep it between the two of you. If he listens to you, you have won your brother over. If he does not listen, summon another, so that every case may stand on the word of two or three witnesses. If he ignores them, refer it to the church. If he ignores even the church, then treat him as you would a tax collector." We often begin to deal with difficulties by treating one another as tax collectors!

My experience is that such sound gospel advice is not observed enough among some parish staffs. We prefer to *talk about* one another rather than *talk to* one another. Such behavior is antithetical to the faith we hold and to which we give our lives in service. More harm is done in parish life by this than by almost any other kind of problem. And the worst thing is that it so often affects the team that is supposed to exist to make the many into one in worship. As *Liturgical Music Today* notes: "Clergy and musicians should strive for mutual respect and cooperation in the achievement of their common goals" (#66).

A second step would be to create clearly defined job descriptions and expectations for both priests and musicians. No one can do or be everything, especially in today's age of specializations. If pastors would learn to delegate administrative tasks, then they would have time to be what people really need from priests: sources of spiritual nourishment in worship, prayer and personal-community relations. Such priests would become less burned-out proprietors and more satisfied pastors. That shift of emphasis may even please the not-easy-to-please musicians.

COMMENTS ON LITURGICAL MUSIC TODAY

Finally, on music and musicians, *Liturgical Music Today* (1983), the supplement to *Music in Catholic Worship* (1972), offers sound principles and guidelines for creating aesthetic liturgies. The document emphasizes that these are not a new set of fixed rules and patterns. "Guidelines, far from being absolute, need to be adapted to particular circumstances. But first they must be read, reflected upon and valued for the insights they contain" (#4). This simply reaffirms *Music in Catholic Worship:* "No set of rubrics or regulations will ever achieve a truly pastoral celebration of the sacramental rites. Such regulations must always be applied with a pastoral concern for the given worshipping community" (#41).

A useful distinction is made between music that accompanies ritual actions and music that stands on its own as "a constituent element of the rite" (#10). In both instances, "the music enriches the moment and keeps it from becoming burdensome" (#9). Accompanying music includes processions: entrance, gospel, preparation and communion; the Lamb of God which accompanies the breaking of bread; music during anointings and vesting at ordinations, etc. Music standing on its own includes acclamations, litanies, songs of praise and the solemn chanting of the eucharistic prayers "In each of these cases the music does not serve as a mere accompaniment, but as the integral mode by which the mystery is proclaimed and presented" (#10).

An interesting new term is introduced in *Liturgical Music Today:* "progressive solemnity." This principle "takes into account the abilities of the assembly, the relative importance of the individual rites and their constituent parts, and the relative festivity of the liturgical day" (#13). Although music is a normal and ordinary part of every celebration, it is not helpful to always sing everything that is singable in a particular celebration. The relative importance of the rites would help determine what is sung on a lesser feast or occasion. The relative abilities of the assembly would also be considered in applying the principle of progressive solemnity. For example, more is sung on a great occasion with a large gathering than is sung at the 7:00 a.m. liturgy on Wednesday of the 31st week in Ordinary Time.

"Liturgical music today must be as diverse and mutli-cultured as the members of the assembly" (#55). Music from the folk idiom, if good music, can be effectively blended with classical hymnody and choral polyphony even in Latin. On the other hand, "a certain integrity within a liturgical prayer or rite" is recommended. For example, eucharistic acclamations should employ only one musical style within an individual celebration. It can be jarring to the ear to hear the presider chant the Gregorian preface, followed by a rock-like "Holy" and moving toward Lucien Deiss's "Keep in Mind" as the memorial acclamation, climaxing with the Danish amen. Unity of musical style within an individual part of the ritual is more conducive to flow and prayer.

The document encourages mixing musical styles, media and languages. At times, however, a celebration using music of only one period or style can be beautiful and effective. There is no reason to bury that "treasure of inestimable value" which is our sacred music from the past. "Singing and playing the music of the past is a way for Catholics to stay in touch with and preserve their rich heritage. A place can be found for this music, a place which does not conflict with the assembly's role and the other demands of the rites" (#52).

For example, a choir might sing a Palestrina or Haydn Gloria. They might also sing a polyphonic setting of the Agnus Dei during communion. A polyphonic setting of the Sanctus, however, should not be sung as the acclamation concluding the preface. This would eliminate the assembly from singing one of its most important parts of the ritual. Sanctus settings, however, may possibly be used as communion motets.

Instrumental music is to be used for more than accompaniment. Its use can also "assist the assembly in preparing for worship, in meditating on the mysteries, and in joyfully professing its passage from liturgy to life" (#58). Such music is not mere decoration, filling up space until the really important things happen. "It is rather ministerial, helping the assembly to rejoice, to weep, to be of one mind, to be converted, to pray" (#58). However, it must never degenerate into idle background music (#59). Silence must also be respected, "and the temptation must be resisted to cover every moment with music" (#59).

Recorded music, while it should not generally replace live music, may be used to accompany singing in outdoor processions and in masses with children. Prerecorded sound tracks of electronic music can also be used with live voices and instruments. Other recorded music may be used occasionally "as an aid to prayer, for example, during long periods of silence in a communal celebration of reconciliation. It may never become a substitute for the community's song, however . . ." (#61).

Finally, *Liturgical Music Today* sings a paean of praise for the ministry of music. It bears quotation as a conclusion to this chapter on music and musicians.

> The entire worshiping assembly exercises a ministry of music. Some members of the community, however, are recognized for the special gifts they exhibit in leading the musical praise and thanksgiving of Christian assemblies. These are the pastoral musicians, whose ministry is especially cherished by the Church (#63).

> What motivates the pastoral musician? Why does he or she give so much time and effort to the service of the church at prayer? The only answer can be that the church musician belongs first of all to the assembly; he or she is a worshiper above all. Like any member of the assembly, the pastoral musician needs to be a believer, needs to experience conversion, needs to hear the Gospel and so proclaim the praise of God. Thus, the pastoral musician is not merely an employee or volunteer. He or she is a minister, someone who shares faith, serves the community, and expresses the love of God and neighbor through music (#64).

> The Church in the United States continues on its journey of liturgical renewal and spiritual growth. . . . The words of Saint Augustine remind us of our pilgrimage: "You should sing as wayfarers do—sing but continue your journey. Do not be lazy, but sing to make your journey more enjoyable. Sing, but keep going" (#74).

15

The Role of The Assembly

"Liturgical renewal is just about over now, isn't it, Father?" That is what a parishioner said to me recently. I suspect that this view may be rather common among many today. After all, we have the new liturgical rites now. Most churches have made some modifications in the shape of their sanctuaries to adapt to the Second Vatican Council's requirements for worship. And almost all churches have brought more and more people from the congregation "up front" to fulfill liturgical ministries. So what is left to be done? The greatest task of all remains ahead of us. It is that of helping the assembly itself fulfill its role in the liturgy.

Liturgical renewal may appear to have been about turning altars around, getting lay people into liturgical ministries, and getting some new books and new music for worship. But that was only the beginning. Worship reform and renewal is actually about turning *people* around, turning the assembly in other directions— namely, toward one another, toward their own individual interior lives and toward the God who is present both within and around them.

The assembly is the true *celebrant* of the eucharist. The priest, rather than being labeled "the celebrant," would better be termed "the presider" at the assembly's worship. As the *General Instruction of the Roman Missal* states in what I consider possibly its most profoundly provocative words: ". . . the whole congregation offers the sacrifice" (#54). The assembly co-celebrates the eucharist.

A profound conversion of vision, relationships and behaviors is envisioned by those words. They speak about the eucharistic prayer, that part of the mass usually associated with the priest alone. Yet the Instruction tells us that even this "center and high point of the entire celebration" is the work of the entire assembly.

The presiding priest speaks the words of the great prayer, not on his own but only in the name of the worshiping assembly present and in the name of the whole church.

But how can assemblies be made more conscious of their role as "celebrants"? How can the people who come to liturgy become aware that what matters most is not so much what goes on "up front" as what happens "all around?" What one sees and what one gets at a liturgy is conditioned by the attitude and the atmosphere created by the entire celebrating assembly.

The answer is both simple and complex. Obviously the members of the assembly must come to *care about being together,* not just being isolated individuals within the same space. That calls for a great deal more than merely fulfilling the Sunday obligation. It means noticing and caring about one another. It involves looking like a group celebrating common spiritual interests and concerns, feeling an energy of reverent hospitality which is drawing them together for prayer and praise. It involves creating spaces for worship which gather people together, not stack them up in front of a sanctuary-stage. It means decorating the entire worship area, not just the platforms for the ambo, altar and presider's chair.

Two other suggestions can be useful. First, parishes need to find ways in which people can become more comfortable with, and more caring about, one another *outside the liturgical gathering place.* What happens in community worship is conditioned at least as much by what happens *between* celebrations as by what happens *during* them. The atmosphere of comfort and caring begins when people feel welcome and respected in the interactions in the parish parking lot, in workplaces and homes, and in the rest of the shared life of the parish. The way the parish lives day-to-day sets the tone and the rhythm for the way the assembly worships. Worship cannot a community make. Communities make worship. At least they must be persons in the process of becoming a Christian community.

Second, we need to help people relax in the worship space. Stiffness and coolness among the members of the assembly cannot energize hospitality. Our traditional reverence at liturgy need not isolate one from the other. We need to learn to balance reverence and hospitality. Many persons and things contribute to this. Chief among them is the joyful and easy (but not buffoon-like) attitude and manner of the presider and other ministers as they welcome people at the entryways of the church before the ritual begins and as they carry out their ministerial roles within the celebration.

The role of the assembly in liturgy may be described as follows:

1) The assembly must *speak the prayers*. Mere physical presence at mass without opening one's mouth scarcely qualifies as full, conscious and active participation. Standing at attention with arms folded and mouths shut, looking like the stone over the tomb on Good Friday is not enough. Worshipers must let the breath out in prayer for the *ruah Yahweh*. The Spirit of God breathing within believers must be let out in prayer.

2) The assembly should *sing the music*. Persons who stand in place, never opening the participation aid, and never singing the psalms, songs and acclamations means that something is seriously missing in that assembly. *All* are invited to lift their voices in song as a way of lifting the words off the pages of the recited texts into truly energized celebrations of faith.

3) The assembly should *be warm and welcoming* toward one another. We must create an atmosphere that makes people feel humanly and spiritually at home with one another in the celebrations.

4) The assembly should *be considerate* of others. This means coming on time, staying until the liturgy ends and trying to minimize distractions and disturbances in the assembly—such as crying children and coughing or whispering adults. I once mentioned "staying until it is over" to a woman and her two children who were being prepared for baptism. I had noticed that they would sit in the back seat at mass and always leave when the people began to receive communion. When I was able to sensitively work this point of Catholic etiquette into the instructions, she said, "Oh, Father Collins, that's just for Catholics isn't it?" Puzzled, I replied, "What do you mean, just for Catholics?" "Well," she said, "I thought when communion time came that we were *supposed to* get up and leave with all of the other non-Catholics in the back of the church."

5) Finally, and most important, the role of the assembly—the presence of believers celebrating together in community—is to *nourish and nurture one another's faith*. Nurturing faith in each of

the members of the assembly is the most important affect and effect of communal worship. "Where two or three are gathered in my name, there am I in their midst," said Jesus.

This point was made quite clear to me when I served as campus minister at Bradley University in Peoria, Illinois, in the early 1970s. There was a senior there named Bob who was, by all accounts, one of the most intelligent, handsome, strong campus leaders around. Bob was a Catholic but did not attend the liturgies. I made it a point to become acquainted with him well enough to ask, "Why don't you join us for mass, Bob?" He told me with great honesty that he used to attend when he was at home with his parents. But he never got anything out of it. Now that he was on his own, he decided that he did not need mass in his life.

I suggested that there was more to mass that just "what you get out of it." It is what you put into it, I said, that enables you to receive something from the experience. Well, that may have been logical to me but it did not appear to persuade Bob. But, about six weeks later, when I was giving the Sunday homily, I noticed Bob was in the assembly. And he was there for the next several weeks as well.

I never found out what brought Bob back—or if he continued to worship as a Roman Catholic. But what I did discover was *how valuable it was for me* to have Bob there in the assembly with us. His presence at mass helped me be present. His efforts to participate helped me want to participate. His struggle to find meaning in the mass supported me in my own efforts to make the mass mean what Christ intended for me and for the assemblies with which I worship. Bob's presence in the assembly helped me be present. His presence and participation nurtured and nourished my own faith.

The question members of worshiping assemblies need to ask themselves is this: Who is "Bob" for you? Whose presence helps you be present? Whose faith helps you believe? Whose faith is sustained by your presence? That nurturance is why two or three gather in Jesus' name. With that sense of the active role of the assembly, the liturgical reform and renewal officially begun at Vatican II can come much closer to fulfillment because liturgy will have become The Art of a Performing Assembly!

Appendix: Liturgy and the Esthetics of John Dewey*

I. THE UNASKED QUESTIONS

Liturgy, according to the Constitution on the Sacred Liturgy of the Second Vatican Council, is an *expression* and an *experience* of two realities: 1) the mystery of Christ; and 2) the nature of the church.[1]

This understanding of worship has guided both the official church and professional liturgists in the liturgical renewal which has followed the Second Vatican Council (1962–1965).

The two words "expression" and "experience" are pivotal concepts both in understanding and in celebrating the renewed liturgy. What forms of expression are most suited to evoke an experience of the mystery of Christ and the nature of the church? What part of the human person is being addressed through these forms of expression? Perhaps the most radical question of all: What is the liturgical experience? Or, to put the question another way, what is the liturgical expressive form supposed to bring about in and for those assembled to worship?

Regrettably, these questions about experience and expressive forms were not faced adequately in the first years of liturgical reform. The questions which did underlie the reform of the rite were those raised by the disciplines of history and theology. Each rite was to be formed "in such a way that the intrinsic nature and

---

*Previously published in *Studia Liturgica*, Volume 18, #2, 1988, pp. 142–160.

purpose of its several parts, as also the connection between them, can be more clearly manifested, and that the devout and active participation by the faithful can be more easily accomplished."[2] It was a reform encouraged and engineered by scholars, based upon academic research of texts.

A new library of liturgical texts has resulted and new liturgical roles have been assumed by members of the worshiping community. But a radical problem remains which can be addressed adequately only if a new kind of question is formulated as a presupposition for the continuing long twilight struggle of liturgical renewal. The new questions will not be based primarily on the scholarly research of historians and theologians, nor even on the multiple questions arising from pastoral practice. The new and more appropriate questions should flow from an examination of the appropriate expressive forms for worship as well as a phenomenological, philosophical exploration of worship's experiential effects upon its creators and participants. To repeat the two previously unasked questions: What part of the human person is addressed and engaged in worship, and what forms of expression accomplish this engagement?

Liturgy, as an expressive form, addresses the human imagination through forms of imagination. Through energized images, symbols, stories and rituals, worship engages *the imaginative system* to know and experience the presence of the mystery of Christ in church and in life. If worship is understood and celebrated in this way, liturgy becomes an art form.

As art, liturgy can be created, composed, choreographed and orchestrated rather than planned. Worship would be woven together much like any artist creates an expressive, esthetic form. Liturgy fails if it is seen primarily as a text to be decorated by the arts of drama, music, poetry and dance. Liturgy can succeed when it is grasped as an art form, subsuming those four arts into itself in a through-composed fashion. To speak of liturgy *and* arts is an unnecessary and unfortunate disjunction. *Liturgy is art.*

If persons are to experience the mystery of Christ present in the church, as Vatican II claims liturgy is meant to do, then this is more likely to occur if liturgy is understood, created and celebrated as an art form, an esthetic expression. The consciousness of more than meets the eye in life, the awareness of mystery, is the work not of that functioning of the mind which we term intellect, but rather of the mind operating as imagination. Through imagination our immediate experience is concentrated and enlarged. "The formal matter of esthetic experience directly *expresses* . . . the meanings that are imaginatively evoked," states John Dewey in *Art as Experience*.[3]

II. ART AS EXPERIENCE

The American philosopher and educator, John Dewey's (1859–1952) classic work, *Art as Experience* (1934), is very useful in exploring the meaning of the thesis that liturgy is an esthetic form of expression. The liturgical experience, both in its creation and in its celebration, is similar to art as an experience. (Keep in mind, as you read Dewey's reflections, that the same insights apply to liturgy.)

Art, according to Dewey, should not be seen as an experience separated from ordinary experience. It is, as a matter of fact, like all experience in that it involves a living being in interaction with environment. As the human organism struggles to both give to and receive from his environment, that person seeks to both put meaning and order into experience and to draw purpose and balance out of experience.

From the dynamic of tensions and resolutions of the most ordinary experience, we seek some integration of past experiences with the newness of the present for the sake of a direction into the future. Memories of the past and anticipations of the future are held in a present balance and a certain equilibrium or simultaneity comes about. In this way experience is unified for the person in interaction with environment and an evolving ordered change or growth is made possible.

All ordinary experience has an esthetic dimension according to Dewey. Art is the expression and the perception of that dimension. Art heightens, deepens and intensifies human experience. It extracts the tensions and resolutions of ordinary experience and highlights them through symbolic form. "Art celebrates with peculiar intensity the moments in which the past reeinforces the present and in which the future is a quickening of what now is."[4]

Art, as a heightened form of experience, can be seen to signify ". . . complete interpenetration of self and the world of objects and events. . . . Because experience is the fulfillment of an organism in its struggles and achievements in a world of things, it is art in germ. Even in its rudimentary forms, it contains the promise of that delightful perception which is esthetic perception."[5]

Such vital, heightened, esthetic experience enables persons to do more than simply relate to reality as observers of causes and effects. Art converts human consciousness to *participate* in reality and to give meaning to all that happens. It also enables the organism to communicate that experience as a matter of consequence and import.

III. THE IMAGINATION

This transformation of the awareness of our experience from observation to participation and communication is facilitated through the operation of the imagination. One way the imagination can be triggered is through the expressive forms of art. The imagination discovers meaning which transcends the senses, analytical logic and discursive reason. Through the imagination, the experience of reality dissolves, diffuses and is re-created. We see and know anew what our experience means.

Fantasy and make-believe are not what is meant by imagination in this context. Imagination is a cognitive power, that moment of knowing in human consciousness when all the powers intersect. Dewey calls this the interaction of inner and outer vision. As this activity takes form in the perceiver of reality, a work of art is born. New possibilities of being-in-the-world are embodied in materials that are not actualized elsewhere. This, Dewey claims, is the synthetic and magical power of imagination which fuses all the faculties together. It is the way in which we know personal, psychic and spiritual truth. Imagination, he says, is

. . . a quality that animates and pervades all processes of making and observation. It is a *way* of seeing and feeling things as they compose an integral whole. It is the large and generous blending of interests at the point where the mind comes in contact with the world. When old and familiar things are made new in experience, there is imagination. When the new is created, the far and strange become the most natural inevitable things in the world. There is always some measure of adventure in the meeting of mind and universe, and this adventure is, in its measure, imagination. . . . An imaginative experience is what happens when varied materials of sense quality, emotion, and meaning come together in a union that marks a new birth in the world.[6]

Drawing upon the evidence of history, Dewey recalls that it has always been through the imagination that matters of the spirit—whether in art or religion—have been expressed. An examination of ritual expression in the Middle Ages, for example, indicates that ". . . the rites and ceremonies of the church were arts enacted under conditions that gave them the maximum possible of emotional and imaginative appeal."[7]

Worship forms that depend not on imagination's expressive forms but on those that primarily address discursive reason will fail to create the conditions of possibility for experiencing mystery in liturgy. " 'Reason' at its height cannot attain complete grasp and a self-contained assurance. It must fall back upon imagination— upon the embodiment of ideas in emotionally charged sense."[8]

Theologies have laid hold on our imaginations through the centuries ". . . because they have been attended with solemn processions, incense, embroidered robes, music, the radiance of colored lights, with stories that stir wonder and induce hypnotic admiration. Most religions have identified their sacraments with the highest reaches of art, and the most authoritative beliefs have been clothed in a garb of pomp and pageantry that gives immediate delight to eye and ear that evokes massive emotions of suspense, wonder and awe."[9]

IV. AN ESTHETIC EXPERIENCE

If art and liturgy have so much in common with ordinary experience, and, indeed, are vital, heightened moments in our experience, then it is useful to distinguish between what is ordinary in our experience and what is esthetic in experience. Dewey calls the latter *"an* experience."[10] Ordinary experience is continuous, but *an* experience is complete in itself, with a beginning and an ending. There is a before and an after.

Such *an* experience has purpose and brings satisfaction. It always involves an esthetic stamp which Dewey claims is an emotional quality. It is an understanding with feeling. This emotional, esthetic quality unifies *an* experience and moves and cements change in the perceiver of the experience.

A unified experience has pattern and structure. It involves a relationship of doing and undergoing. It is both done by the person and something to which the person must surrender in order to have *an* experience. ". . . doings and perceptions projected in imagination interact and mutually modify one another."[11]

Insofar as an experience is controlled by the felt relations of tension and release, order and fulfillment, they become experiences dominantly esthetic in their development. "Every work of art follows the play of, and the pattern of, a complete experience, rendering it more intensely and concentratedly felt."[12]

One who has *an* esthetic experience must do more than *recognize* what happens. That person must also *perceive* what is expressed. Recognition simply acknowledges what is seen without arousing a vivid consciousness of the reality experienced. It does not involve truly energized interaction between the organism and the environment. Perception, on the other hand, is what happens in *an* experience. It is an act of reconstructive doing. It engages the imagination of the perceiver to know with emotion, evoking a seeing of the old in a new way. Such perception is possible only when a certain resistance is expressed between the old and the new so that one may have a consciousness of an experience.

This esthetic phase of experience involves a surrender to that experience on the part of both the creator and the perceiver. It is an ". . . act of the going-out of energy in order to receive, not a withholding of energy. . . . For to perceive, a perceiver must create his own experience. And his creation must include relations comparable to those which the original producer underwent."[13]

Both the creation and the perception of a work of art are acts of expression. They begin with what Dewey terms "an impulsion."[14] This involves a turning outward and forward of the organism in relating to its environment so that a resistance ensues. The old and the new, the past and the present are brought into tension. A re-flection on the old and new takes place like an incubation. From this re-flection, expression flows forth not as an emotional outburst but as a reflective awareness of meaning and purpose. In an act of expression, "an activity that was 'natural' . . . is transformed because it is undertaken as a means to a consciously entertained consequence."[15] Natural materials are employed embodying meaning beyond but within themselves.

Transformation involves a dialectic between present and past experiences. "What is expressed will be neither the past events that have exercised their shaping influence nor yet the literal existing occasion. It will be, in the degree of its spontaneity, an intimate union of the features of present existence with the values that past experience have incorporated in personality. Immediacy and individuality, the traits that mark concrete existence, come from the present occasion; meaning, substance, content, from what is embedded in the self from the past."[16]

Emotion is obviously a key factor in the expressive act. It ". . . operates like a magnet drawing to itself appropriate material: appropriate because it has an experienced emotional affinity for the state of mind already moving. . . . Emotion is informed and carried forward when it is spent indirectly in search for material and in giving it order, not when it is directly expended."[17] This is never raw emotion but emotion reworked in the imagination of the artist-perceiver. It is neither insufficient emotion which ". . . shows itself in a coldly 'correct' product," nor excessive emotion which ". . . obstructs the necessary elaboration and definition of parts."[18]

Expressive acts secure their artistic, emotional, esthetic quality by reworking the raw material of experience. "In this process the emotion called out by the original material is modified as it comes to be attached to the new material."[19] In this expressive, creative process, both the creator and the work of art become transformed. Turbid emotions are clarified and, in the mirror of the created expressive form, our desires and emotions know themselves and, in this esthetic knowing, they are transfigured.

V. ART AS TRANSFORMATIVE EXPRESSION

What happens in art is not a pictorial, literal representation of ordinary experience from the past and present. A selection of aspects of experience is made and then transformed in the perceptions of the artist and perceiver-participant. Both can enter into new relationships with their environment with a new emotional response. When art functions in this fashion in a community, not only is the individual changed but group experience is also renewed in the direction of greater order and unity. The work of art tells something to those who enjoy it about the nature of their own experience of the world. It presents the world in a new experience which artist and perceiver undergo by surrendering to the esthetic qualities of the experience. A new sense of reality is born. "The work of art has a unique quality. . . . It is that of clarifying and concentrating meanings contained in scattered and weakened ways in the material of other experiences."[20]

The product of every expressive act is an expressive object, Dewey says. The expressive object differs radically from a statement which is the product, not of the mind functioning as imagination, but of discursive reason. The statement explains an experience; the expressive object explores it and discloses its inner nature as perceived by the artist and proposed to the perception of the perceiver-participant. The statement is a sign, pointing to a reality other than itself; an expressive object is a symbol that makes present aspects of the reality-experience which it re-presents. The statement gives the meaning of an experience; the expressive object yields the significance, the import. The statement directs to an experience, whereas the expressive object constitutes *an* experience in itself. The statement is prosaic and esthetic. The statement makes known an intention, whereas the expression immediately realizes the intention. The statement indicates meaning; the expressive object contains its meaning.

Art allows persons to see, not fixed and unalterable visions and values in life experience, but new meanings of experience are disclosed for perception. Perceivers-participators can be emancipated from such prejudice as ". . . the intrinsic qualities of things come out with startling vigor and freshness just because conventional associations are removed."[21]

Just as the expressive object can disclose hidden meanings, so also the material of our experience, because of familiarity, prejudice, and conceit, can conceal the expressiveness of ordinary experience. "Art throws off the covers that hide the expressiveness of experienced things; it quickens us from the slackness of routine and enables us to forget ourselves by finding ourselves in the delight of experiencing the world about us in its varied qualities and forms. It intercepts every shade of expressiveness found in objects and orders them in a new experience of life."[22]

The expressive act which results in the esthetic, expressive object is *sui generis*. General material is formed into esthetic substance and the perception of the form and substance varies from person to person and time to time. Although expressive objects may remain the same, as in a painting, a symphony, or a drama, they are, nevertheless, re-created every time they are esthetically perceived. There is a certain multivalent and polysemous character about these expressive forms which permit them to be experienced anew each time they are expressed.

VI. RHYTHM IN ESTHETIC EXPRESSION

The organization of the energies in a work of art depends upon the creation of a sense of rhythm in the expressive object. Each of the parts of an art work must ebb and flow into and out from one another. Each moment is rhythmed toward the next and from the last.

> Thus . . . perception will be serial in order to grasp the whole and each sequential act builds up and reenforces what went before. . . .
>
> There can be no movement toward a consummating close unless there is a progressive massing of values, a cumulative effect. This result cannot exist without conservation of the import of what has gone before. Moreover, to secure the needed

continuity, the accumulated experiences must be such as to create suspense and anticipation of resolution. Accumulation is at the same time preparation, as with each phase of the growth of a living embryo. Only that is carried on which is led up to; otherwise there is arrest and break. For this reason consummation is relative; instead of occurring once for all at a given point, it is recurrent. The final end is anticipated by rhythmic pauses, while that end is final only in an external way.

Such characteristics as continuity, cumulation, conservation, tension and anticipation are thus formal conditions of esthetic form.[23]

The rhythm of the expressive object, with its tensions and releases, reflects ". . . as a substratum in the depths of the subconscious, the basic pattern of the relation of the live creature to his environment."[24] The resistances of rhythm must be brought into a kind of unity. This can happen ". . . only when the resistances create a suspense that is resolved through cooperative interaction of the opposed energies."[25] It is the resistance between old and new experienced in esthetic experience which ". . . defines the place of intelligence in the production of an object of fine art. A rigid predetermination of an end-product whether by artist or beholder leads to the turning out of a mechanical or academic product. The consummatory phase of experience . . . always presents something new. Admiration always includes an element of wonder."[26]

It is this sense of awe and wonder which must be retrieved in liturgy if it is to be an experience of mystery. With this wonder-ful power, the liturgical experience does not cease when the direct act of perception stops. It becomes a seed within consciousness which will not decay except to grow into ever-new awareness of the depths of experience.

The organization of esthetic energies involves the creator and the perceiver in feelings about the substance thus formed. An art work does not communicate primarily to or through discursive reason. It engages the mind in its imaginative functioning in an experience of perceived truth through the beauty of form with its attendant feelings. The force of such a work is in the interpenetration of qualities and relations as perceived with feeling and completeness of form. "We cannot grasp any idea, any organ of meditation, we cannot possess it in its full force, until we have felt it and sensed it, as much so as if it were an odor or a color. . . ."[27]

The matter and energy of art is so organized that the unseen becomes perceived. "Through art, meanings of objects that are otherwise dumb, inchoate, restricted, and resisted are clarified and concentrated, and not by thought working laboriously upon them, not by escape into a world of mere sense, but by creation of a new experience. . . . But whatever path the work of art pursues, it, just because it is a full and intense experience, keeps alive the power to experience the common world in its fullness. It does so by reducing the raw materials of that experience to matter ordered to form."[28]

All arts have in common the organization of energy. All involve the interpenetration of the material by the rhythm. When the rhythms are perceived, there is esthetic experience. Depths of meaning and vitality are disclosed, both in the art work itself and in the active process of perception. What is perceived is not simple recurrence, one thing after another, but rather relationships carried forward. The relationships of the elements and energies recur in differing contexts and with different consequences so that each recurrence is novel as well as a reminder. "Every closure is an awakening, and every awakening settles something. This state of affairs defines organization of energies."[29]

Such organization of energies, such interaction of elements, move and stir, calm and tranquilize perceivers. Different senses perceiving the art work function in relation to one another. The energies of one expressive form are communicated to other centers of expression and ". . . new modes of motor responses are incited which in turn stir up new sensory activities."[30] The energies compressed from prior life experiences and esthetic experiences and perceptions into the present experience are impulsed forward with intensity into the future. Such compression is produced by selecting the potencies in things which give *an* experience significance and value. Those potencies are then organized in their multiple resistances until an art work is produced which involves both rhythm and symmetry.

Rhythm and symmetry cannot be separated. "When intervals that define rest and relative fulfillment are the traits that especially characterize perception, we are aware of symmetry. When we are concerned with movement, with comings and goings rather than arrivals, rhythm stands out."[31]

The artistic imagination reaches out beyond limits externally set by the material used ". . . so that the value of that material may be pressed out and become the matter of a new experience."[32] These elements blend and fuse into a unity which physical things can only emulate. The penetrating quality which unites the individual parts into a rhythmed whole can only be emotionally intuited. "But without the intuited enveloping quality, parts are external to one another and mechanically related. Yet the organism which is the work of art is nothing different from its parts or members. It *is* parts as member. . . ."[33]

VII. THE MEDIUM AND ITS PERCEIVER

In addition to the organization of energies, all arts share a common substance, namely, a medium or a vehicle of expression in space and time. "The important thing is that a work of art exploit *its* medium to the uttermost—bearing in mind that material is not medium save when used as an organ of expression."[34] "Whenever any material finds a medium that expresses its value in experience— that is, its imaginative and emotional value—it becomes the substance of a work of art."[35]

A work of art is not just the product of an artist. It becomes a work of art when ". . . a human being cooperates with the product so that the outcome is an experience that is enjoyed because of its liberating and ordered properties."[36] All of the impressions made must be integrated into a single perception and the integrating, synthesizing agent is the mind functioning as imagination. This is the organic push from within which turns a product of art into a work of art.

The word mystical is sometimes attached to such experiences of the extraordinary disclosed within the ordinary. This same word is often associated with the experience of a work of art. It can involve the seen revealing the unseen, the understood disclosing the incomprehensible. "Every work of art must have about it something *not understood* to obtain its full effect."[37] What is sensed, yet not completely understood, is that the esthetic experience elicits and accentuates a perception of belonging to a reality larger than the self, an all-inclusive whole which is the universe in which we live. This helps to explain the religious, awesome feeling that often accompanies intense esthetic perception. "We are, as it were, introduced into a world beyond this world which is nevertheless the deeper reality of the world in which we live in our ordinary experiences. We are carried out beyond ourselves to find ourselves."[38]

Those words of John Dewey, perhaps to Dewey's surprise, can be seen as echoing the vision of Jesus: to be in the world but not of the world; to find oneself, one must be willing to lose oneself. In Christian worship, as in any work of art, expressive forms operate ". . . to deepen and to raise to great clarity that sense of an enveloping undefined whole that accompanies every normal experience. This whole is then felt as an expansion of ourselves."[39]

VIII. LITURGY AS ESTHETIC EXPRESSION/EXPERIENCE

Life experiences can become more intelligible through participation in a liturgy created and celebrated as an esthetic experience. However, this intelligibility is not that of reflection and science which renders things more intelligible by reduction to conceptual form. Rather, intelligibility is disclosed by presenting meaning ". . . as the matter of a clarified, coherent, and intensified or 'impassioned' experience."[40]

The knowledge gained through involvement in liturgy as art is knowing transformed. It is ". . . something more than knowledge because it is merged with non-intellectual elements to form *an* experience worthwhile as an experience."[41]

The efficacy of liturgical celebrations, from the point of view of both the creator and the perceiver of such expressive forms, depends primarily upon the degree in which the human imaginative system is engaged. Dewey recalls that the church has, at its best, connected art with human experience, weaving a fabric of real life with its esthetic rituals. Because of this, he contends, "religious teachings were the more readily conveyed and their effect was the more lasting. By the art in them, they were changed from doctrines into living experiences."[42] The texts become events for a celebrating people.

Liturgy, like art, is a work of the human imagination, heightening and intensifying ordinary experience. It is *an* experience. Through its expressive forms, worship can clarify our experience and concentrate its meanings through symbolic action. This must involve an interaction between the persons who create/celebrate liturgy and the environment of their lived experience. Liturgy must be related to life, not only on the surface but, more significantly, in its deepest streams.

If, as Dewey claims, life is an art in germ, one might suggest life is also liturgy in germ. Every experience, if it is *an* experience in Dewey's sense, contains the quality of mystery for those with eyes to see and ears to hear. Every significant moment bears ritual potential: birth, coming of age, meals, marriage, conversion, illness and death, to name only some of life's major moments. Through esthetic forms engaged in by a believing community, *an* experience becomes possible, one which is complete with a clear beginning and ending and one which bears the esthetic quality of feeling.

Persons who do and undergo ritual, with its tensions and resolutions, can experience a catharsis in which the imagination purges the feelings of threat and gloom and opens the possibility of a deep sense of confidence and trust. New possible modes-of-being-in-the-world are disclosed as projects for the imagination to create and to hope in.

This can happen very effectively at a wedding when a material form such as a candle engages the imagination of those in love. It can communicate a deep experience of love's root meanings to those who surrender to participate in the ritual. The preacher would explore the symbol by saying: "This candle is like you and me. It has all it takes to be a candle—wax, wick, shape, color, odor—but it lacks something that alone will make it truly what it is. It needs a spark from outside itself, a gift of flame. Then it will give off light and warmth. Then it will be what it is meant to be."

We are like that. We have all it takes to be human beings. Yet, we need a gift, a spark of love from our God—a gift mediated usually through other persons and events. Then we glow. Then we become warm and give off light. Before that we are as incomplete as the unlighted candle.

But there is more to the symbol. When the candle receives the gift of flame, it does not only give off light and warmth. The flame also sears and burns and consumes the candle in the very process of becoming its true self. So with us. The gift of flame that lights us with love and holiness, once received, if not quenched, will not only make us givers of light and warmth into the world, it also will burn and consume us and, like the candle, perhaps we will be only truly ourselves when we are all gone up in smoke.

Used in a homily, such a simple symbol can turn listeners into participants in the mystery of their own lives. It gives them the space to walk around and find themselves. It can move them toward a commitment, a consummation in faith.

IX. ACTIVE PERCEPTION IN LITURGY

Participation in worship's esthetic expressions, like perception in art, is the important concept here. Observers of the liturgy can be led, through such symbolic expression, to become active participants, not just moving their lips but being moved in their imaginations. A kind of knowing takes place by imagination, by sympathetic engagement. Each one finds in the *polysemous* character of the symbol a meaning unique to the self at that moment. The esthetic expressive form, energizing senses and, emotion, communicate unified meaning which can be like a new birth.

A key to such imaginative engagement, to participation, is found in Dewey's distinction between recognition and perception. Perception is energized interaction. It is a doing and an undergoing which Dewey terms a reconstructive doing. Those who create and celebrate liturgy let go of enough of their understanding of their experience to allow new meanings to enliven and re-create old experiences and understandings. This involves, of course, the rhythm of resistance, a kind of tug and pull between old and new, out of which the new vision comes and the commitment is cemented.

Our sense of time can be touched in a liturgy created and celebrated as an art form. Past, present and future collapse into a single now in which some integration of past experiences with the present comes about for the sake of a direction in the future. Our experience, through the simultaneity and equilibrium of imagining, becomes unified as memories of the past and anticipations of the future are held in a present balance.

A man angry at his mother-in-law attended a Sunday liturgy in which the gospel of the prodigal son was read. Until the words of that familiar story were not just heard and *recognized* but *perceived* by the frustrated man, he had only been rehearsing his history of mother-in-law horror stories. But when he let go of those memories enough to listen to the Jesus story, he found that story to be his own. Through imagination's functioning, he walked around in the space of the story and the prodigal became himself. In that simultaneity he saw that he had to try again to come home and make attempts at reconciliation. The tension between his remembered story and the familiar but newly heard Jesus story made possible and energized resolution and he went out and tried again. Memories of the past and anticipations of the future achieved a present balance. Such is the potential of esthetically energized ritual.

The primary past event made present in each liturgy is, of course, the paschal mystery, the death and resurrection of Jesus. The liturgy re-presents that originating event just as any work of art is grounded in a past experience. This is the root metaphor of Christianity. All experience for a believer in Jesus is lived and interpreted in the light of this faith-event. Even though it was a once-for-all event, in the expressive object of liturgy, that event becomes present again for those who surrender to the symbolic action of the ritual. It becomes not just the experience of Jesus and past Christians but it is presented for present perception so that perceivers-participants may make that experience of dying and rising their own. It can ". . . enable them to have more intense and more fully rounded out experiences of their own."[43] That is what Dewey calls form with substance. Such a work is matter formed into esthetic substance which is immediate to the perceivers experience.

X. CREATING AND CELEBRATING LITURGY AS ART

The responsibility of the liturgical artist is to shape the ritual materials so that the worshipers' past and present experiences can be brought into an immediate, clear perception, giving insight with feeling into the deepest dimensions of both past and present with directions into the future. The personal elements and the material of the ritual are ". . . organically absorbed into the perception had here and now. They give it its body and its suggestiveness. They often come from sources too obscure to be identified in any consciously memorial way, and thus they create the aura and penumbra in which a work of art swims."[44] In liturgy, for example, the participant-perceiver must experience something of the originating event of the ritual and of the process of creation which produced the esthetic ritual event. The one who composed the ritual begins with the esthetic "impulsion" of which Dewey speaks. The interaction of the artist with experience is done under the pressure of impulsion. Life and liturgy converge in the artist's imagination. A kind of incubation period must take place in the liturgist in which "what is conceived is brought forth and is rendered perceptible as part of the common world."[45] What distinguishes the esthetic dimension in *an* experience is the "conversion of resistance and tensions, of excitations that in themselves are temptations to diversion, into a movement toward an inclusive and fulfilling close."[46]

In the incubation period of creativity, the raw experience and raw emotion perceived in the original impulsion are reworked in the imagination. The artist intercepts shades of expressiveness and nuances of meaning. The liturgist who is an artist will extract and select particular traits and dimensions of the object to be expressed. This selection is based upon the interest of the artist arising from his own integrated experience and from his perception of the interests and needs of the community for whom the work of art is being created. New possible modes-of-being-in-the-world are thereby disclosed as projects for the imagination. What may be inconceivable can be revealed as real and possible.

In this truly creative approach to preparing liturgy, the artist who creates it uses material reality to express perceived truth with feeling. The forms embody the transformed insight of the artist who is changed by creating the art work, the liturgy. This transformation happens through surrender to the esthetic qualities of the liturgy being composed. There must be in that person the same new awareness of the mystery of human life and its meaning as is present when any artist creates.

If such transformative vision happens for a liturgy's creator, then, through the expressive forms created, conditions of possibility for transformation can become available for participants' perception and transformation. In such a way, then, the creator of the liturgy, the artist, is an exegete and an interpreter of others' ordinary experience.

The expressive object called liturgy must create for worshipers the conditions of possibility for exploring the meaning of their human experience in light of Christianity's root metaphor. It can do so by making that meaning present as a symbolic esthetic expression which contains what it signifies for those who surrender to undergo the experience of the expressive object.

As in any art work the medium expresses the meaning and the value of the experience. The imagination becomes energized to see more than meets the eyes of sense and discursive reason. To quote Dewey again: "Whenever any material finds a medium that expresses its value in experience—that is, its imaginative and emotional value—it becomes the substance of a work of art."[47] The esthetic material needs to be exploited to the uttermost.

In liturgy, as in art, the unseen is seen with feeling. The understood discloses the incomprehensible. The esthetic experience of eucharist elicits and accentuates a perception of belonging to a reality larger than the self. "We are, as it were, introduced into a world beyond this world which is nevertheless the deeper reality of the world in which we live our ordinary experiences. We are carried out beyond ourselves to find ourselves."[48]

XI. THE RHYTHM OF RITUAL

All of this is possible in worship as an esthetic expressive form through an esthetic organization of the energies that comprise the ritual moments. There must be within the liturgy an ebb and flow of parts in which the parts are experienced as a whole, not just a succession of parts. Such esthetic expression and perception demands rhythm in ritual, similar to the consumption and release that comprise the rhythm in any art work. Rhythm is the organization of the energies of ritual.

Rhythmed energy is what can transform ritual texts into celebrations, words into events. Dewey, you will recall, compared this to the phases of growth in an embryo, "Only that is carried on which is led up to. . . ."[49] A progressive massing of values moves toward a cumulative close. With the creation of suspense and anticipation, consummation is not given only at one point but rather is recurrent throughout. "The final end is anticipated by rhythmic pauses. . . ."[50]

The matter of ritual, to become energized and the bearer of spiritual meaning, must become interpenetrated with rhythm. What is perceived by participants is relationships of parts carried forward to a consummative close. The entrance rite energized toward the liturgy of the word; the profession of faith and the general intercessions tapers off from the high moments of the word service; the preparation of gifts climaxes in the eucharistic prayer and communion rite with a closure in the dismissal rite. Such an awareness of the rhythms of eucharistic ritual can create the conditions of possibility for experiencing the mystery of Christ as the expressed meaning of ordinary experience. As Dewey says of art, the matter is "pressed out" through rhythmed movement and becomes the matter of new experience.[51] The elements of liturgy blend and fuse into a unity which matter can only emulate. The penetrating enveloping quality which joins the parts into a whole is the imagination, emotionally intuiting the one out of the many. Without this imaginative perception, liturgy, like art, remains as only parts external to one another, only mechanically related.

The distinction Dewey draws between a statement and an expressive, esthetic object is helpful in addressing the problem of overly verbal and conceptual liturgies. We need to make liturgy less a statement and more of an esthetic expression. To summarize Dewey, on the other hand, the *statement* explains in prosaic, scientific fashion. It points to something other than itself in the manner of a sign, indicating the meaning of an experience and making known an intention. On the other hand, the *expressive object,* in poetic and esthetic fashion explores and symbolizes, making immediately present the reality it represents. It contains its meaning which is yielded as significance. The esthetic object constitutes an experience in itself.

XII. LITURGY AND THE WORLD

Liturgy, created and celebrated as an art form, could become an elitist experience for the comfortable. It could possibly be misinterpreted as related only to the church's self-identity and intramural experience. It could be utterly unworldly. Nothing could be further from the goal of esthetic worship, however.

Liturgy as an esthetic experience can open perceivers to a sense of being part of a larger whole, an all-inclusive whole which is the universe in which we live. Liturgies celebrated esthetically can energize believers, individually and communally, to see more than self-interest in lived experience and to become instruments for bringing God's kingdom of justice and peace into the world. In rhythmed ritual, the stirrings of dissatisfaction with the present social order and its systemic sin as well as intimations of a better future are found. Here, new and more just images-of-being-in-the-world cluster in imaginations and are disclosed as possibilities. These changes in the climate of the imagination become precursors of changes in social existence, changes that affect more than just the details of life but touch the substance as well.

It is the imagination which Dewey claims to be ". . . the chief instrument of the good."[52]

"A man to be greatly good must imagine intensely and comprehensively," he says. "The first intimations of wide and large redirections of desire and purpose are of necessity imaginative. Art is a mode of prediction not found in charts and statistics, and it insinuates possibilities of human relations not to be found in rule and precept, admonition and administration." "Art has been the means of keeping alive the sense of purposes that outrun evidence and of meanings that transcend indurated habit."[53]

Liturgy as art has the potential both for creating more celebrative Christian communities and for stimulating a vision and a motive for establishing that kingdom of truth and life, of holiness and grace, that kingdom of justice, love and peace which is in but not of this world. This liturgical power can be activated through forms of esthetic expression which engage the imagination to know life as mystery.

NOTES

1. This is the teaching of the *Constitution on the Sacred Liturgy*, #2, promulgated by the Second Vatican Ecumenical Council in December, 1963.
2. *Ibid.*, #50.
3. John Dewey, *Art as Experience*, (New York: Minton, Balch & Co., 1934), p. 273.
4. *Ibid.*, p. 18.
5. *Ibid.*, p. 19.
6. *Ibid.*, p. 267.
7. *Ibid.*, p. 31.
8. *Ibid.*, p. 33.
9. *Ibid.*, p. 30.
10. *Ibid.*, Chapter III.
11. *Ibid.*, p. 52.
12. *Ibid.*, p. 52.
13. *Ibid.*, pp. 53–54.
14. *Ibid.*, Chapter IV.
15. *Ibid.*, p. 62.
16. *Ibid.*, p. 71.
17. *Ibid.*, pp. 69–70.
18. *Ibid.*, p. 70.
19. *Ibid.*, p. 74.
20. *Ibid.*, pp. 83–84.
21. *Ibid.*, p. 95.
22. *Ibid.*, p. 104.
23. *Ibid.*, pp. 136–138.
24. *Ibid.*, p. 150.
25. *Ibid.*, p. 161.
26. *Ibid.*, pp. 138–139.
27. *Ibid.*, p. 119.
28. *Ibid.*, p. 138.
29. *Ibid.*, p. 169.
30. *Ibid.*, p. 175.
31. *Ibid.*, p. 179.
32. *Ibid.*, p. 189.
33. *Ibid.*, pp. 192–193.

34. *Ibid.*, p. 228.
35. *Ibid.*, p. 229.
36. *Ibid.*, p. 214.
37. *Ibid.*, p. 194.
38. *Ibid.*, p. 195.
39. *Ibid.*, p. 195.
40. *Ibid.*, p. 290.
41. *Ibid.*, p. 290.
42. *Ibid.*, p. 329.
43. *Ibid.*, p. 109.
44. *Ibid.*, p. 123.
45. *Ibid.*, p. 56.
46. *Ibid.*, p. 56.
47. *Ibid.*, p. 229.
48. *Ibid.*, p. 195.
49. *Ibid.*, p. 137.
50. *Ibid.*, p. 138.
51. *Ibid.*, p. 189.
52. *Ibid.*, p. 348.
53. *Ibid.*, pp. 348–349.